Backgammon Board

WIN AT BACKGAMM

3 x 340g packets buttercake mix
2 quantities Vienna cream
¾ cup cocoa
500g packet white soft icing
red and black colourings
pure icing sugar
8 licorice straps
assorted sweets

Make cakes according to directions on packets. Divide mixture evenly between 2 greased 20cm x 30cm lamington pans. Bake in moderate oven for about 40 minutes or until firm; cool on wire racks.

STEP 1

Place cakes side by side on prepared board, join cakes with a little Vienna cream. Stir sifted cocoa gradually into remaining cream, spread over cakes.

STEP 2

Tint half the soft icing red, knead in a little sifted icing sugar if icing is sticky. Roll icing on surface dusted with sifted icing sugar to a 10cm x 17cm rectangle. Cut into 12 x 2.8cm x 10cm triangles. Roll out and cut remaining soft icing into the same sized triangles as red icing.

Arrange licorice strips and triangles on cake. Make dice from scraps of icing, mark with black colouring. Decorate cake with sweets and dice.

Table from The Country Trader; chair from Wentworth Antiques

3

Ballet Points

3 x 340g packets buttercake mix
1 quantity fluffy frosting
1 quantity Vienna cream
blue and rose pink colourings
3 metres gold braid
narrow pink ribbon

Make cakes according to directions on packets. Divide mixture evenly between 2 greased 15cm x 25cm loaf pans and greased 23cm square slab pan. Bake in moderate oven for about 40 minutes or until firm; cool on wire racks.

STEP 1

Use paper pattern to cut ballet points from loaf cakes.

STEP 2

Hollow out ballet points from shapes. Position slab cake on prepared board. Tint fluffy frosting blue, spread over slab cake, decorate with braid. Tint Vienna cream pink, spread over ballet points. Place points on cake, decorate with ribbon.

Dolls from Martinvale

4

Banana Split

3 x 340g packets buttercake mix
2 quantities fluffy frosting
1 sponge roll
yellow, rose pink and brown
    colourings
chocolate-flavoured Ice Magic
2 wafer biscuits
red glace cherries
marshmallows

Make cakes according to directions on
packets. Two-thirds fill 3 greased muffin
pans (⅓ cup capacity) with mixture.
Spread remaining mixture into greased
32cm long oval cake pan. Bake cakes in
moderate oven for about 20 minutes,
remove small cakes. Bake large cake
about further 40 minutes or until firm; cool
cakes on wire racks.

STEP 2

Cut sponge roll into quarters
lengthwise; trim 1 end of each quarter to a
curved shape.

Place oval cake on prepared board,
spread with half the frosting, reserve
¼ cup frosting. Tint two-thirds of remaining frosting yellow.

STEP 1

Scoop out centre of oval cake, leaving
3cm edge. Discard cake scraps.

STEP 3

Spread sponge roll lengths with yellow
frosting, position on cake as shown.

STEP 4

Spread 1 small cake with reserved
white frosting. Divide remaining frosting in
half, tint pink and brown. Spread remaining cakes with both frostings. Lift cakes
into position on bananas. Decorate with
Ice Magic, wafers, cherries and
marshmallows.

Basketball

3 x 340g packets buttercake mix
2 quantities Vienna cream
orange colouring
2 licorice straps

Make cakes according to directions on packets. Divide the mixture between 2 greased and floured aluminium pudding steamers (9 cup capacity, or with 20cm diameter top and 9½cm depth). Bake in moderate oven for about 1 hour or until firm; cool on wire racks.

Level tops of cakes, sandwich together with a little Vienna cream; position on prepared board. Tint remaining cream orange, spread cakes with cream. Cut licorice into thin strips, arrange on cake.

Bears' Brunch

2 x 340g packets buttercake mix
85g packet quandong jelly crystals
1 cup boiling water
green colouring
2 quantities Vienna cream
2 cups green coconut
1 licorice strap
assorted sweets
1 toy umbrella
250g packet chocolate caramel bears
2 x 250g packets chocolate Milk
   Batons

Make cakes according to directions on packets. Spread mixture into greased 32cm long oval cake pan. Bake in moderate oven for about 40 minutes or until firm; cool on wire rack.

Make jelly using the 1 cup of boiling water, refrigerate until set.

STEP 1

Level top of cake, position on prepared board. Tint Vienna cream green, spread evenly over cake. Sprinkle with coconut. Cut 30cm length of licorice strap. Push licorice into surface of cake, leaving 1cm above surface to outline pool.

Chop jelly finely, spoon some into licorice circle for pool.

STEP 2

Make slippery-dip using sweets and licorice. Decorate cake with the remaining ingredients.

Bears in cars from Teddy & Friends

Beautiful Butterfly

2 x 340g packets buttercake mix
3 sponge rollettes
2 quantities Vienna cream
black, yellow and blue colourings
2 licorice straps

Make cakes according to directions on packets. Spread mixture into greased 32cm long oval cake pan. Bake in moderate oven for about 40 minutes or until firm; cool on wire rack.

Cut oval cake in half lengthways. Position rollettes end to end on prepared board, join with a little Vienna cream; shape ends of butterfly's body. Position wings, secure with a little cream.

Tint quarter of remaining cream black, spread over body. Tint quarter of the remaining cream yellow, tint remaining cream blue.

Spread blue and yellow creams onto wings. Cut licorice into thin strips, use for feelers and to outline and decorate wings.

Billiard Table

3 x 340g packets buttercake mix
2 sponge rolls
3 quantities Vienna cream
green and brown colourings
1 long thin licorice tube
shredded coconut
1 pretzel stick
assorted sweets

Make cakes according to directions on packets. Spread mixture evenly into 3 greased 20cm x 30cm lamington pans. Bake in moderate oven for about 30 minutes or until firm; cool on wire racks.

STEP 3

Cut centre out of the remaining cake, leaving a 2cm border. Discard centre of cake. Place border on top of green cream.

STEP 1

Cut each sponge roll into 3 pieces, position on prepared board to support top of table.

STEP 4

Spread inside of border with reserved green cream. Tint remaining cream brown, spread over remaining cake.

STEP 2

Spread a little Vienna cream on top of each table leg. Sandwich 2 cakes together, position on top of table legs. Tint quarter of the remaining cream green; spread three-quarters over top cake, reserve remaining quarter.

STEP 5

Decorate cake with remaining ingredients, using coconut for the pockets.

Accessories from MacIntosh Gibbs Pty Ltd

Calculator

2 x 340g packets buttercake mix
2 quantities Vienna cream
blue and black colourings
2 licorice straps
3 licorice allsorts

Make cakes according to directions on packets. Spread three-quarters of the mixture into greased 20cm x 30cm lamington pan and remaining mixture into greased 8cm x 26cm bar pan. Bake cakes in moderate oven for about 30 minutes, remove bar cake. Bake lamington cake for about further 10 minutes or until firm; cool cakes on wire racks.

STEP 3

Cut piece of bar cake diagonally. Position cakes on prepared board, join with a little Vienna cream. Reserve ¼ cup of the cream. Tint one-third of the remaining cream blue. Tint remaining cream grey, using black colouring.

Spread grey cream evenly over sides, back and slope of calculator. Spread blue cream evenly over top of calculator.

Use licorice and pieces of licorice allsorts for keys. Pipe on keys with reserved cream.

STEP 1

Cut 5cm from a long side of the lamington cake.

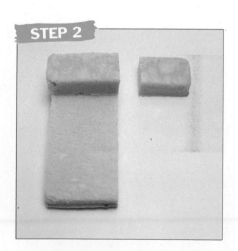

STEP 2

Place bar cake on lamington cake, cut to the same width.

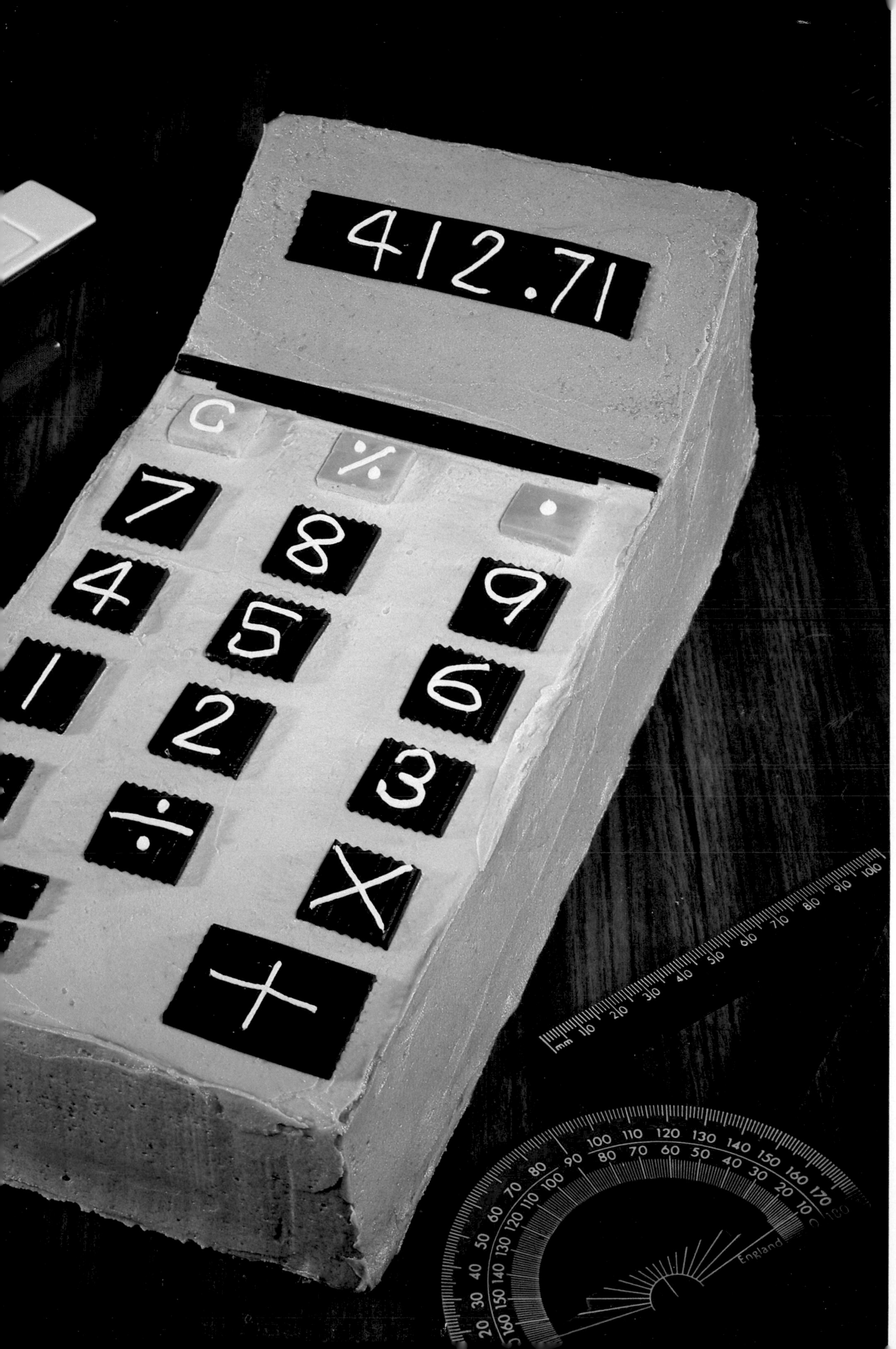
412.71
C
%
7
8
9
4
5
6
1
2
3
England

Chess Board

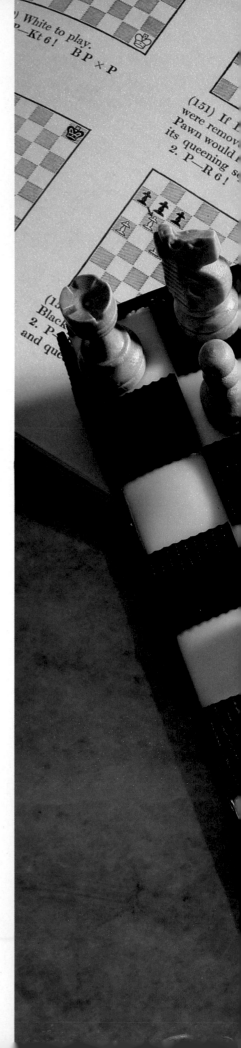

340g packet buttercake mix
8 licorice straps
1 quantity Vienna cream
500g packet white soft icing
1 cup pure icing sugar, approximately

Make cake according to directions on packet. Spread mixture into greased 23cm square slab pan. Bake in moderate oven for about 35 minutes or until firm; cool on wire rack.

Cut out 32 squares of licorice.

STEP 2

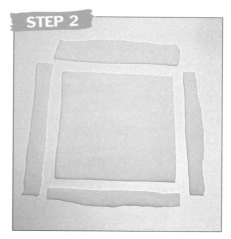

Knead soft icing with a little sifted icing sugar until icing loses its stickiness. Roll out icing on surface lightly dusted with sifted icing sugar, slightly larger than top of cake. Trim icing to fit top of cake exactly, carefully lift soft icing onto cake.

Press licorice squares gently into icing. Position remaining lengths of licorice around sides of cake.

STEP 1

Trim sides of cake to make square. Place cake on prepared board. Spread cake evenly all over with Vienna cream.

Chic Top Hat

3 x 340g packets buttercake mix
2 quantities Vienna cream
rose pink colouring
3 licorice straps
feathers

Make cakes according to directions on packets. Spread 2 cups of the mixture into greased deep 28cm round cake pan. Divide remaining cake mixture between 2 greased deep 17cm round cake pans. Bake cakes in moderate oven for about 15 minutes, remove large round cake. Bake remaining 2 cakes for about further 40 minutes or until firm; cool on wire racks.

STEP 2

Decorate hat with licorice band and feathers. Make a bow from licorice, secure to cake with toothpick.

STEP 1

Level tops of cakes, sandwich together on prepared board with a little Vienna cream. Tint remaining cream pink, spread evenly all over cakes.

Chocolate Block

340g packet buttercake mix
1 quantity Vienna cream
brown, blue, yellow and red
   colourings
1 licorice strap
500g block Top Deck chocolate

Make cake according to directions on packet. Spread mixture into greased 20cm x 30cm lamington pan. Bake in moderate oven for about 30 minutes or until firm; cool on wire rack.

STEP 2

Spoon red cream into piping bag, pipe outline of large letters, fill in with cream. Outline a band across the chocolate block with thin strips of licorice, fill in with yellow cream, pipe in letters. Spread remaining cake with brown cream. Decorate cake with chocolate pieces and foil.

STEP 1

Place cake on prepared board. Cut a groove diagonally across cake. Reserve 1 cup Vienna cream, tint two-thirds of the remaining cream chocolate brown, tint remaining cream blue. Tint 2 tablespoons of reserved cream yellow and remaining cream red. Spread lower section of cake evenly with blue cream.

Chunk of Cheese

2 x 340g packets buttercake mix
1 quantity Vienna cream
red and yellow colourings
8 White Melts
½ cup shredded coconut, toasted
small round coloured sweets
1 licorice strap

Make cakes according to directions on packets. Place paper patty cases into 3 muffin pans (⅓ cup capacity), two-thirds fill each paper case with mixture. Spread remaining mixture into greased deep 28cm round cake pan. Bake cakes in moderate oven for about 20 minutes, remove small cakes. Bake large cake for about further 20 minutes or until firm; cool cakes on wire racks.

Sandwich cake wedges together with a little Vienna cream, place on prepared board. Reserve ⅓ cup of the remaining cream for mice. Tint two-thirds of the remaining cream red, spread over curved side and top of cake. Tint remaining cream yellow, spread over flat sides of cake. Decorate with White Melts.

Cut cake into 3 even-sized wedges.

Remove paper cases from small cakes, cut cakes in half crossways, join halves together with a little of the reserved cream. Spread cakes with remaining reserved cream, roll cakes in coconut. Decorate with sweets and licorice.

Clumsy Clown

2 x 340g packets buttercake mix
2 quantities Vienna cream
1 sponge rollette
red, green, yellow and orange
   colourings
2 long thin licorice tubes
assorted sweets
pink and white marshmallows
¼ cup shredded coconut, toasted
1 small red ball
ribbon

Make cakes according to directions on
packets. Divide mixture between greased
25cm long oval cake pan and greased
deep 23cm round cake pan. Bake cakes
in moderate oven for about 30 minutes or
until firm; cool on wire racks.

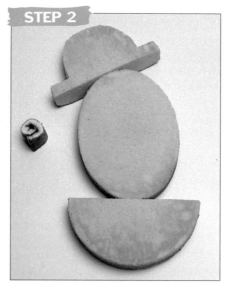

STEP 2

Position cut-out cakes and oval cake
on prepared board; join pieces with a little
Vienna cream. Position rollette for hat's
decoration.

Spread half the remaining cream
evenly over oval cake and rollette. Tint half
the remaining cream red, spread evenly
over hat and mouth. Divide remaining
cream into 3 portions, tint each portion
with green, yellow and orange colourings.
Spread portions over collar. Decorate
cake with remaining ingredients.

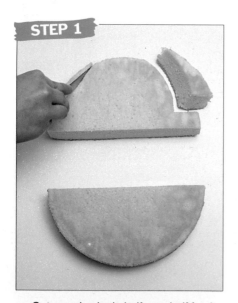

STEP 1

Cut round cake in half, use half for the
collar, cut hat from remaining half.

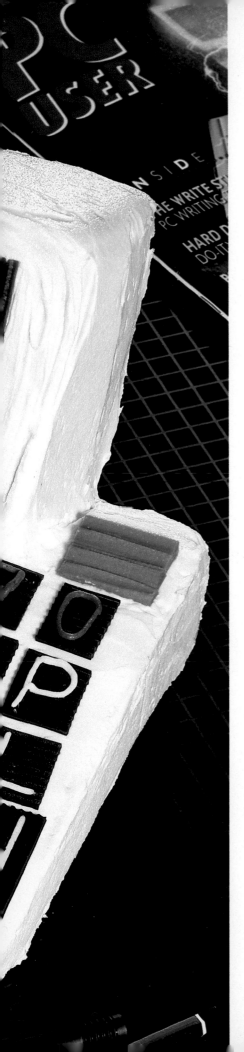

Computer

3 x 340g packets buttercake mix
2 quantities Vienna cream
2 thin wooden skewers
black and rose pink colourings
3 musk sticks
6 licorice straps

Make cakes according to directions on packets. Spread half the mixture into greased 20cm x 30cm lamington pan, spread remaining mixture into greased 14cm x 21cm loaf pan. Bake cakes in moderate oven for about 40 minutes, remove lamington cake. Bake loaf for about further 15 minutes or until firm; cool on wire racks. Level top of loaf cake.

STEP 2

Place half the cake on prepared board, join remaining half of lamington cake with a little Vienna cream so that the 2 narrow sides are joined.

STEP 1

Split lamington cake diagonally in half to represent keyboard.

STEP 3

Position loaf cake for screen, using skewers to hold in position.

Tint 1 cup of the remaining cream grey with black colouring, spread evenly over screen. Reserve ½ cup of the remaining cream, spread remaining cream evenly over remaining cake. Decorate cake with musk sticks and licorice.

Tint half the reserved cream pink, use for piping numbers, etc. Pipe letters onto licorice with remaining cream.

Crossword Puzzle

340g packet buttercake mix
4 licorice straps
1 quantity fluffy frosting
licorice allsorts
1 teaspoon egg white
½ cup pure icing sugar,
   approximately
rose pink colouring

Make cake according to directions on packet. Spread mixture into greased 23cm square slab pan, bake in moderate oven for about 35 minutes or until firm; cool on wire rack.

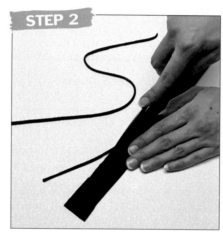

STEP 2

Cut remaining licorice into thin strips. Place cake onto prepared board. Spread cake evenly with frosting.

STEP 1

Cut half the licorice into squares.

STEP 3

Decorate cake with licorice squares and strips and letters cut from pieces of licorice allsorts. Beat egg white lightly in cup with teaspoon, gradually beat in sifted icing sugar until icing is thick and pipable. Tint icing pink, spoon into piping bag, pipe numbers into corners.

Table from The Country Trader

Cruiser

3 x 340g packets buttercake mix
2 quantities Vienna cream
2 small ice-cream cones
green, orange, yellow and blue
    colourings
assorted sweets
thin wooden skewer
cotton wool
4 licorice straps

Make cakes according to directions on packets. Divide two-thirds of the mixture into 2 greased 15cm x 25cm loaf pans, divide remaining mixture into 2 greased 8cm x 26cm bar pans. Bake cakes in moderate oven for about 30 minutes, remove bar cakes. Bake loaf cakes about further 10 minutes or until firm; cool cakes on wire racks.

STEP 3

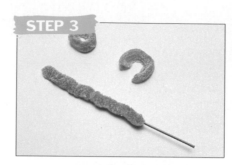

Use remaining plain cream for tops of decks and funnels, use the different colours for decorating the rest of the cruiser. Make mast by threading soft jellies onto wooden skewer, place in position on cruiser. Decorate cruiser with sweets, cotton wool and licorice strips.

STEP 1

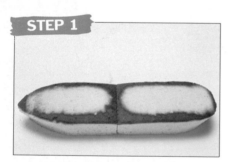

Level tops of loaf cakes, trim ends, join ends with a little Vienna cream, place onto prepared board. Trim cake to shape.

STEP 2

Use trimmed bar cakes to make upper decks, join cakes together with a little cream. Make funnels with trimmed cones.

Tint 1½ cups cream green, tint 1 cup cream orange, tint ¾ cup cream yellow, tint ¼ cup cream blue.

Background painting from Prop Art, Sydney

Cuddly Koala

3 x 340g packets buttercake mix
2 quantities Vienna cream
thin wooden skewers
2 Golden Roughs
rose pink and black colourings
1 licorice strap
1 white marshmallow
2 small round black sweets

Make cakes according to directions on packets. Pour two-thirds of the mixture into greased and floured aluminium pudding steamer (11 cup capacity, or with 19cm diameter top and 11½cm depth).

Two-thirds fill 2 greased muffin pans (⅓ cup capacity) with mixture, spread remaining mixture into greased and floured aluminium pudding steamer (6 cup capacity, or with 15cm diameter and 9½cm depth). Bake cakes in moderate oven for about 20 minutes, remove small cakes. Bake small round cake about further 15 minutes. Bake large round cake about further 30 minutes or until firm; cool cakes on wire racks.

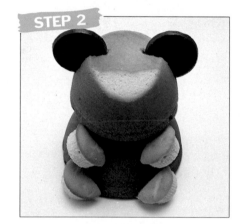

STEP 2

Cut slits in top cake, position Golden Roughs for ears. Tint 2 teaspoons of the remaining cream pink for mouth. Reserve ⅔ cup of cream.

Tint remaining cream grey, using black colouring, spread evenly over cake and ears, except for tummy and centres of ears. Spread reserved cream over tummy and ears. Use pink cream for mouth. Decorate with remaining ingredients.

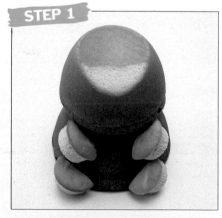

STEP 1

Level tops of large cakes, join together with a little Vienna cream; place on prepared board. Cut small cakes in half crossways, attach to body with skewers.

Dannie Dinosaur

2 x 340g packets buttercake mix
2 quantities Vienna cream
green colouring
200g packet spearmint leaves, halved
assorted sweets
1 licorice strap

Make cakes according to directions on packets. Divide mixture between 2 greased 20cm x 30cm lamington pans, bake in moderate oven for about 30 minutes or until firm; cool on wire racks.

Position cake pieces together on prepared board; join with a little Vienna cream. Tint remaining cream green; spread evenly all over cake.

Place cakes side by side, use paper pattern to cut out dinosaur.

Mark in scales with spatula. Decorate cake with remaining ingredients.

Dice

2 x 340g packets buttercake mix
2 quantities Vienna cream
yellow colouring
licorice straps
small round coloured sweets

Make cakes according to directions on packets. Divide mixture between 2 greased 23cm square slab pans. Bake in moderate oven for about 35 minutes or until firm; cool on wire racks.

STEP 1

Cut 1 cake into quarters, trim sides. Cut remaining cake in half. Discard 1 half of cake, cut other half into 2 squares, trim sides. You need 6 squares for this cake.

STEP 2

Sandwich 3 squares of cake together with a little Vienna cream. Repeat with remaining squares. Slice a corner from 1 dice so dice will sit flat. Place dice on prepared board. Tint cream yellow, spread evenly all over cakes. Decorate cakes with thinly sliced licorice and sweets.

Fairy Queen

2 x 340g packets buttercake mix
2 quantities Vienna cream
1 large chocolate coin, halved
red, yellow and blue colourings
silver cachous
assorted sweets

Make cakes according to directions on packets. Spread mixture into 2 greased 20cm x 30cm lamington pans. Bake in moderate oven for about 30 minutes or until firm; cool on wire racks.

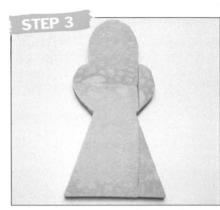

STEP 3

Join pieces of cake together with a little Vienna cream, assemble fairy queen on prepared board. Use a little more cream to outline face. Cover coin halves with a little cream; reserve coin halves for hands.

Tint 3 teaspoons of cream pink, use to highlight cheeks. Tint 1 cup of cream yellow, use for hair. Tint remaining cream blue, spread over remaining cake.

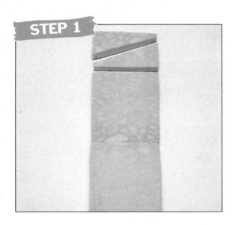

STEP 1

Place cakes together, end to end. Cut 2 wedges from end of 1 cake.

STEP 4

Position hands, decorate cake with remaining ingredients. Position cut-out cardboard wings. Cover wings with fabric if desired. Make wand from wood and glitter-covered cardboard star, if desired; position as shown.

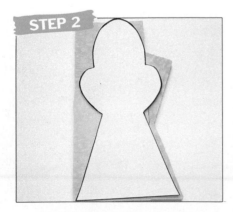

STEP 2

Position cake wedges at side of cake. Use paper pattern to cut out fairy queen.

Background painting from Prop Art, Sydney

Froggy

We used quandong (see Glossary) and lime jellies to make Froggy's pond. When making the jellies, use only half the water stated on the packet. After they are set, chop them roughly and mix them for a pretty effect.

2 x 340g packets buttercake mix
2 quantities Vienna cream
green and red colourings
2 licorice straps
coloured sweets
1 wafer biscuit

Make cakes according to directions on packets. Spread mixture into 2 greased 20cm x 30cm lamington pans. Bake in moderate oven for about 30 minutes or until firm; cool on wire racks.

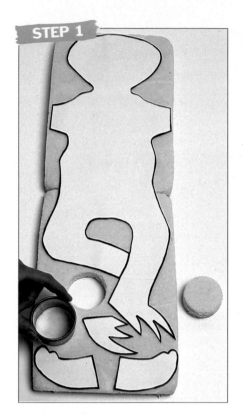

STEP 1

Position cakes end to end. Use paper pattern to cut out cakes. Cut out eyes using 5cm cutter.

STEP 2

Position cake pieces together on prepared board, join with a little Vienna cream. Use toothpicks to secure Froggy's overlapping foot.

Tint half the remaining cream green, use for body. Tint half the remaining cream red, use for shorts. Use remaining plain cream for Froggy's shirt and eyes. Decorate cake with licorice, sweets and piece of wafer biscuit for tongue.

Waterlilies from Ledora Farm

Gorgeous Gorilla

4 x 340g packets buttercake mix
3 quantities Vienna cream
brown colouring
2 licorice straps
black jelly beans
chocolate sprinkles
bow tie

Make cakes according to directions on packets. Divide mixture evenly between 3 greased 20cm x 30cm lamington pans and greased 23cm square slab pan. Bake cakes in moderate oven for about 35 minutes or until firm; cool on wire racks.

STEP 2

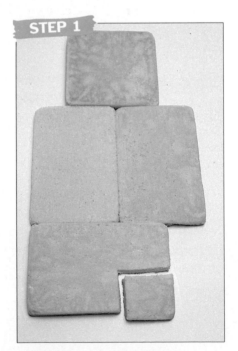

STEP 1

Position cakes and cut as shown.

Use paper pattern to cut out gorilla, assemble on prepared board, join pieces with a little Vienna cream.

Tint quarter of the remaining cream pale brown, use for face. Tint remaining cream dark brown, spread evenly over remaining cake. Decorate cake with remaining ingredients.

Halloween Horror

2 x 340g packets buttercake mix
2 quantities Vienna cream
yellow and purple colourings
½ cup cocoa
plastic skeleton
yellow sweets

Make cakes according to directions on packets. Divide mixture between greased 15cm x 25cm loaf pan and greased 20cm x 30cm lamington pan. Bake cakes in moderate oven for about 30 minutes; remove lamington cake. Bake loaf cake for about further 10 minutes or until firm; cool cakes on wire racks.

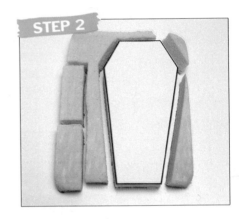

Use same paper pattern to cut lid from lamington cake, cut pieces from trimmings for end of coffin.

Cut top from loaf cake, discard top. Use paper pattern to cut out cake (end of coffin is cut from lamington cake).

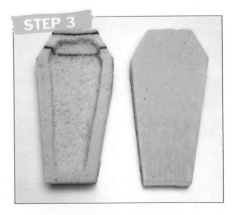

Assemble coffin from base of loaf cake and trimmings from lamington cake on prepared board, join with a little Vienna cream. Hollow out coffin, about 1cm deep, leaving 1cm edge. Tint ½ cup Vienna cream yellow. Tint 1 cup of the remaining cream purple. Beat sifted cocoa into remaining cream.

Spread lid and sides of coffin with chocolate cream. Spread inside of coffin with purple cream.

Pipe yellow cream onto lid. Place skeleton into coffin, top with lid; decorate sides of coffin with sweets.

Hamburger

340g packet buttercake mix
1 cup flaked coconut
green, brown, black, red and yellow
   colourings
2 quantities Vienna cream
2 Flakes, crushed
green and red sweets
2 teaspoons sesame seeds, toasted

Make cake according to directions on packet. Spread mixture into greased deep 23cm round cake pan. Bake in moderate oven for about 35 minutes or until firm; cool on wire rack.

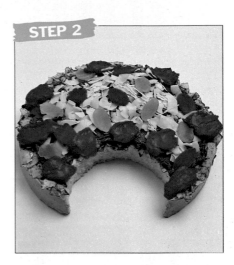

STEP 2

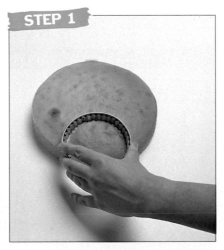

STEP 1

Place lower half of cake onto prepared board, spread with reserved cream, spread side of bun with half the caramel cream, top cake with green coconut. Spread hamburger patty mixture over coconut, leaving a 1cm border. Sprinkle with remaining white coconut, then green sweets, then red sweets.

Drop spoonfuls of red cream around side and cut edge of cake for tomato sauce. Top bun with top half of cake, spread side with remaining caramel cream, spread top with darker brown cream; sprinkle with sesame seeds.

Cut semi-circle from cake, using 10cm round fluted cutter. Split cake in half horizontally. Tint ¾ cup of the coconut green. Tint one-third of the Vienna cream with a combination of brown, black and red colourings to make hamburger patty; stir in Flakes. Reserve 2 tablespoons of the cream.

Tint 2 tablespoons of the remaining cream red. Tint ¾ cup cream a caramel colour with yellow and brown colourings for side of bun. Tint remaining cream slightly darker for top of bun.

Glasses from Vasa Agencies

Hoppy Kangaroo

4 x 340g packets buttercake mix
3 quantities Vienna cream
6 thin wooden skewers
1 small ice-cream cone
4 sponge rollettes
4 Wagon Wheels
brown, yellow and red colourings
1 licorice strap
1 black jelly bean

Make 3 cakes according to directions on packets. Spread 2 cups of the mixture into greased 8cm x 26cm bar pan, pour remaining mixture into greased and floured Dolly Varden cake pan (10 cup capacity, or with 18cm diameter top and 15cm depth).

Bake cakes in moderate oven for about 30 minutes; remove bar cake. Bake large cake about further 45 minutes or until firm; cool on wire racks.

Make remaining cake, spread mixture into greased deep 17cm round cake pan. Bake in moderate oven for about 45 minutes or until firm; cool on wire rack.

STEP 2

Place round of cake on body, secure in position with skewers. Shape head from remaining piece of bar cake, place into position on skewers.

STEP 4

Cut 3 of the rollettes in half lengthways, position and trim rollettes for tail, joining with a little cream. Sandwich Wagon Wheels together in pairs with a little cream, place on sides of cake for thighs. Cut the remaining rollette in half lengthways, use for feet.

Reserve ¼ cup of the cream. Tint remaining cream with a combination of brown, yellow and red colourings to give a reddish-brown, spread over cake and back of ears. Roughen with a fork.

Tint reserved cream with the same colourings to give a paler reddish-brown. Spread over pouch area and inside ears. Decorate cake with licorice and jelly bean for Hoppy's nose.

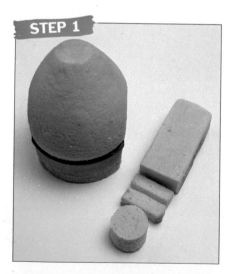

STEP 1

Join round cake and Dolly Varden cake together with a little Vienna cream, trim sides for thighs. Cut 5½cm diameter round from 1 end of bar cake, cut 15cm piece from other end of cake for head. Cut remaining cake piece in two for arms.

STEP 3

Halve ice-cream cone lengthways; cut to shape for ears, press gently into head, secure with skewers. Place short skewers into remaining cake slices for arms. Position cake on prepared board.

Background painting from Prop Art, Sydney

Icy Igloo

2 x 340g packets buttercake mix
1 quantity fluffy frosting
3 x 250g packets white marshmallows
1 licorice strap

Make cakes according to directions on packets. Spread three-quarters of the mixture into greased and floured aluminium pudding steamer (8 cup capacity, or with 18cm diameter top and 9½cm depth). Spread remaining cake mixture into greased 8cm x 26cm bar pan. Bake cakes in moderate oven for about 30 minutes, remove bar cake. Bake large cake about further 30 minutes or until firm; cool cakes on wire racks.

Cut bar cake in half crossways; discard 1 half. Trim sides of bar cake to make rounded like a tunnel. Cut away a little cake for tunnel's entrance. Level top of round cake.

Position cakes on prepared board, join with a little frosting. Spread remaining frosting evenly over cake. Cover cake with marshmallows. Outline igloo entrance with a thin strip of licorice.

Jack in the Box

4 x 340g packets buttercake mix
4 quantities Vienna cream
4 plain doughnuts
red, yellow, green, blue, purple and
rose pink colourings
assorted sweets
1 licorice strap
tinsel

Make cakes according to directions on packets. Two-thirds fill 2 greased muffin pans (⅓ cup capacity) with mixture. Divide remaining mixture between 4 greased 23cm square slab pans. Bake cakes in moderate oven for about 20 minutes; remove small cakes. Bake slab cakes about further 15 minutes or until firm; cool cakes on wire racks.

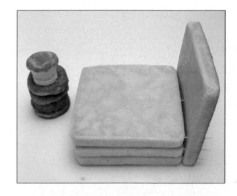

Join 3 square cakes together with a little Vienna cream, position on prepared board. Place remaining square cake in position for lid; secure with toothpicks.

Join doughnuts together with a little cream. Cut 2cm slice from 1 small cake; discard slice. Top doughnuts with small cakes; join with a little cream.

Tint half the remaining cream red, spread over square cakes. Divide remaining cream into 5 portions, tint each portion with the remaining colours. Spread doughnuts with different coloured creams, spread pink cream over head. Position doughnut stack on cake. Decorate cake with remaining ingredients.

Toys from Martinvale

55

Joe Bad

3 x 340g packets buttercake mix
2 quantities Vienna cream
rose pink, black, purple, yellow, blue,
**   red, green and orange colourings**
2 licorice straps

Make cakes according to directions on packets. Spread mixture into 2 greased 20cm x 30cm lamington pans. Bake in moderate oven for about 40 minutes or until firm; cool on wire racks.

STEP 2

Mark hairline and stubble using a bunch of toothpicks dipped into liquid black colouring. Decorate cake with licorice, studs, earring and pins, if desired.

STEP 1

Place cakes together, use paper pattern to cut out cakes. Position cakes on prepared board, join pieces with a little Vienna cream.

Tint half the remaining cream pale rose pink; reserve 2 tablespoons. Spread remaining pink cream evenly over face, except for mouth, glasses and hair. Divide remaining cream into 7 portions, colour each portion with the remaining colours. Make glasses with some of the black cream. Make lips with purple cream.

Tint reserved rose pink cream a darker pink, spoon into piping bag, pipe outlines for nose, ear and jaw.

Make spiked hair with different coloured creams, run a toothpick through hair to create texture.

Belts from Let It Rock Shop; background from Prop Art, Sydney

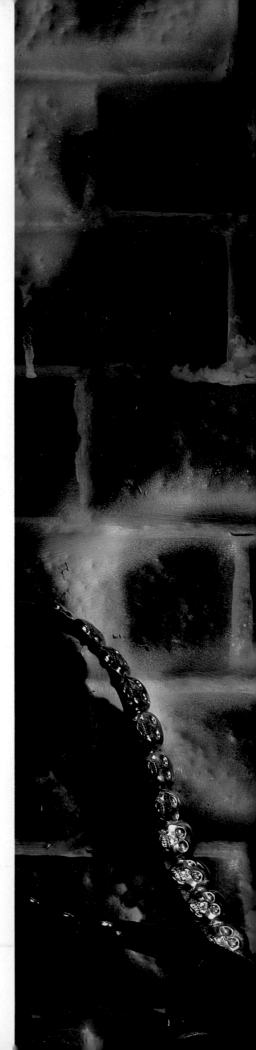

56

Kitty Cat

3 x 340g packets buttercake mix
2 quantities Vienna cream
brown, orange and green colourings
2 licorice straps

Make cakes according to directions on packets. Spread mixture into 2 greased 20cm x 30cm lamington pans. Bake in moderate oven for about 40 minutes or until firm; cool on wire racks.

Place cakes together, use paper pattern to cut out cakes. Position cakes on prepared board, join pieces with a little Vienna cream.

Tint three-quarters of the remaining cream with a combination of brown and orange colourings to make a ginger colour. Tint 2 tablespoons of the remaining cream green.

Spread ginger cream over body, use plain cream for chest, paws and inside ear. Roughen with spatula. Use green cream for eyes. Use licorice strips to outline features, whiskers, etc.

Magic Cube

2 x 340g packets buttercake mix
2 quantities Vienna cream
red, green, blue, orange and yellow
    colourings
3 licorice straps

Make cakes according to directions on
packets. Divide the mixture between
3 greased deep 15cm square cake pans.
Bake in moderate oven for about 30
minutes or until firm; cool on wire racks.

   Level cakes, position cakes on
prepared board, join together with a little
Vienna cream. Using a sharp knife, mark
9 squares on the 5 exposed sides of the
cube. Divide remaining cream into 6 portions, tint 5 portions with the different
colours, leave 1 portion plain.
   Carefully colour in squares on cake
with the different creams. Cut licorice
straps into 3mm strips; use to divide
colours on cube.

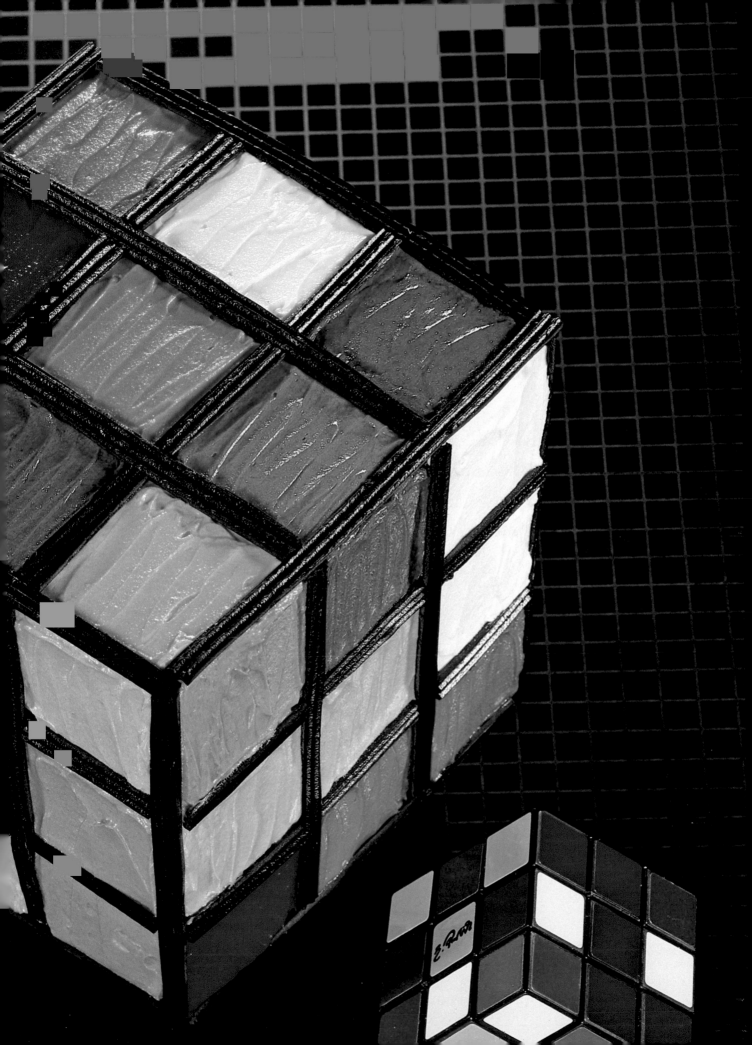

Marina

2 x 340g packets buttercake mix
2 x 85g packets quandong jelly
    crystals
2 quantities Vienna cream
yellow colouring
5 licorice straps
green shredded coconut
assorted sweets
5 plastic boats (about 10cm long)

Make cakes according to directions on packets. Spread mixture into greased deep 28cm round cake pan. Bake in moderate oven for about 45 minutes or until firm; cool on wire rack.

Make jellies according to directions on packets, pour into lamington pan, refrigerate until firm; mash with fork.

STEP 1

Split cake in half horizontally, cut small pieces from each cake so the cakes fit together. Join cakes on prepared board with a little Vienna cream.

STEP 2

Position pieces of cake on 1 side of 1 cake to make a wall, join with a little cream. Tint remaining cream yellow, spread all over cake. Decorate cake with jelly, licorice, coconut, assorted sweets and boats.

Party Patty Cakes

Little Bert has the tiger; little Lizzie has the piglet! You can use these party patty cakes instead of place cards or you can make a variety of them for fun. Grown-up kids will love them also.

Here are some of our ideas to inspire your own party patty cakes.

To make about 24 cakes, you'll need a 340g packet of buttercake mix, 1 quantity of Vienna cream, assorted colourings and a variety of sweets.

Make buttercake according to directions on packet. Place paper patty cases in muffin pans (1/3 cup capacity). Two-thirds fill paper cases with mixture, bake in moderate oven for about 20 minutes or until firm; cool on wire rack. Colour Vienna cream as desired, decorate cakes with cream and assorted sweets.

LANKY

SPINNER

SPARKY

SPRING BLOSSOMS

SPRING BASKET

TUFFY TIGER

KIM KOALA

SMILEY

BABY BEAR

GLAMOUR PUSS

PINKY PIGLET

RASCAL RABBIT

RING-A-LING

TUSKY

Medieval Castle

85g packet quandong jelly crystals
1 cup boiling water
3 x 340g packets buttercake mix
2 quantities Vienna cream
250g packet sponge rollettes
black colouring
¼ cup chocolate sprinkles
250g packet chocolate Mint Batons
1 long thin licorice tube
1 licorice strap
plastic toys
green shredded coconut

Make jelly as directed on packet, using the 1 cup of boiling water; cool, refrigerate until set.

Make cakes according to directions on packets. Spread mixture into 2 greased deep 23cm round cake pans. Bake in moderate oven for about 50 minutes or until firm; cool on wire racks.

Cut a 1cm deep 10cm x 12cm square from side of cake for entrance.

Position cakes on prepared board, join with a little Vienna cream, top with 7 sponge rollette halves, secure rollettes with a little more cream.

Tint remaining cream dark grey with black colouring; reserve ¼ cup cream. Spread dark grey cream evenly over cake except for entrance to castle. Tint reserved cream black, spread over entrance. Mark brick work on side of cake with toothpick or skewer. Decorate top of cake with chocolate sprinkles.

Surround cake with chopped jelly for moat. Use batons and licorice tube for drawbridge, and licorice strap for windows. Decorate castle with toys and shredded coconut.

67

Music Box

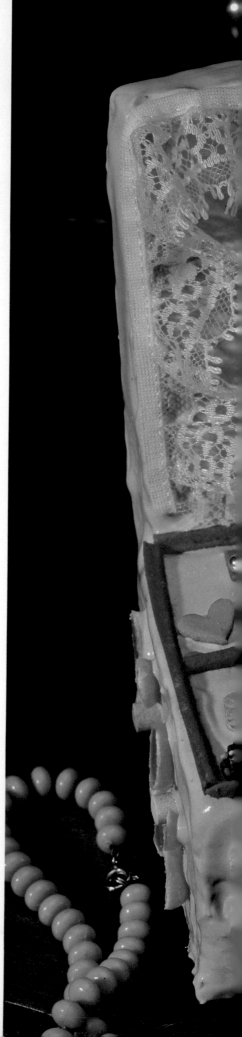

2 x 340g packets buttercake mix
3 thin wooden skewers
1 quantity fluffy frosting
rose pink colouring
30cm lace trim
small mirror
small plastic ballerina
assorted sweets

Make cakes according to directions on packets. Spread three-quarters of the mixture into greased 14cm x 21cm loaf pan. Bake in moderate oven for about 55 minutes or until firm; cool on wire rack. Remaining mixture can be baked at the same time in patty pans or bar pan for another use.

Position cakes on prepared board, secure lid with skewers. Tint frosting pink, spread evenly over cake. Decorate cake with remaining ingredients.

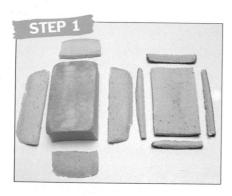

Cut a 2cm horizontal slice from top of loaf cake for lid. Trim sides from both pieces of cake to make straight sides.

Noah's Little Ark

We used quandong jellies for water (see Glossary) and Rocky Road for cliffs.

4 x 340g packets buttercake mix
3 quantities Vienna cream
yellow and orange colourings
2 x 150g packets Chocolate Stiks
**   Biscuits**
thin chocolates
1 licorice strap
sweets
plastic toys

Make cakes according to directions on packets. Spread mixture into 3 greased 14cm x 21cm loaf pans. Bake in moderate oven for about 55 minutes or until firm; cool on wire racks.

Place triangles on either side of remaining cakes; cut cakes to ark shape.

Cut a 5cm slice from each end of 1 cake, cut small triangular pieces from slices as pictured; discard scraps of cake.

Position pieces of cake on prepared board; join with a little Vienna cream. Tint two-thirds of the remaining cream yellow; spread evenly over top and sides of ark shape. Cut remaining piece of loaf cake to shape for house; position on ark with a little cream. Tint remaining cream orange; spread evenly over house cake.

Decorate side of ark with Chocolate Stiks and thin chocolates for roof and ramp. Use licorice and sweets for door and windows. Position toys.

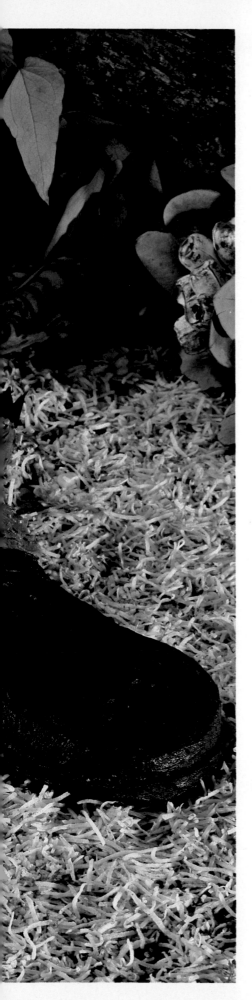

Perry Platypus

We used quandong jellies for water (see Glossary).

3 x 340g packets buttercake mix
2 quantities chocolate Vienna cream
black colouring
1 white marshmallow
2 small round sweets
1 licorice strap
green shredded coconut

Make cakes according to directions on packets. Divide two-thirds of the mixture between 2 greased 15cm x 25cm loaf pans. Spread remaining mixture into greased deep 23cm round cake pan. Bake cakes in moderate oven for about 30 minutes, remove round cake. Bake loaf cake about further 10 minutes or until firm; cool on wire racks.

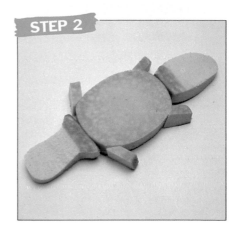

Position cakes together on prepared board, join with a little Vienna cream. Cut feet from cake scraps, position with cream. Cut bill and tail to shape.

Tint quarter of the remaining cream with black colouring to make dark brown, spread over bill. Spread remaining chocolate cream over rest of body, roughen with fork. Mark nostrils and opening in bill. Decorate cake with the remaining ingredients.

Place cakes side by side, use paper pattern to cut out platypus.

Petal Panda

3 x 340g packets buttercake mix
1½ quantities fluffy frosting
black colouring
1 licorice strap
14 slivered almonds
1 licorice allsort
red ribbon

Make cakes according to directions on packets. Spread 2 cups of the mixture into greased 8cm x 26cm bar pan. Divide remaining mixture between 2 greased 23cm square slab pans. Bake cakes in moderate oven for about 30 minutes; remove bar cake. Bake slab cakes about further 15 minutes or until firm; cool cakes on wire racks.

STEP 2

Use paper pattern to cut out cakes.

STEP 1

Level bar cake to the same height as the slab cakes; position cakes together.

STEP 3

Use scraps from bar cake to fill in the gaps. Join pieces of cake together with a little frosting on prepared board.

Tint half the remaining frosting black. Spread black and white frosting over cake. Decorate cake with licorice pieces, almonds, coloured pieces of licorice allsort and a red ribbon bow.

Pineapple

2 x 340g packets buttercake mix
2 quantities Vienna cream
green, yellow and orange colourings
3 licorice straps

Make cakes according to directions on packets. Spread mixture into 2 greased 23cm square slab pans. Bake in moderate oven for about 35 minutes or until firm; cool on wire racks.

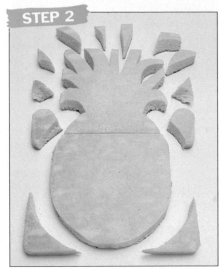

Join cakes on prepared board with a little Vienna cream.

Place cakes together, use paper pattern to cut out cakes.

Use cake scraps to extend leaves, secure in position with a little more cream.

Divide remaining cream into 3 portions, tint each portion with a different colour. Spread green cream over leaves and yellow cream over base of pineapple. Spoon orange cream into piping bag fitted with small fluted tube, pipe stars on cake. Outline cake with licorice strips and dots.

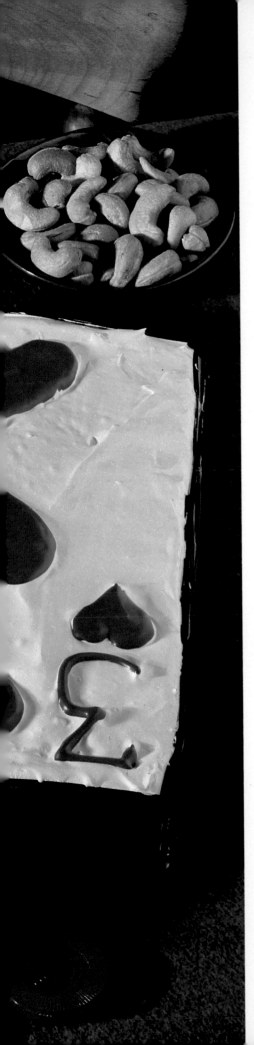

Playing Cards

3 x 340g packets buttercake mix
1 quantity fluffy frosting
4 licorice straps
red and black colourings

Make cakes according to directions on packets. Spread mixture into 2 greased 20cm x 30cm lamington pans. Bake in moderate oven for about 40 minutes or until firm; cool on wire racks.

Cut a diagonal strip from the centre of 1 cake, as shown.

Position cakes on prepared board, secure with a little frosting. Use the strip of cake to fill in the gaps. Spread three-quarters of the remaining frosting evenly over cakes. Cut 1 licorice strap into thin strips, use to outline cards. Use remaining straps around sides of cake.

Divide remaining frosting into 2 portions, tint red and black. Mark numbers and shapes on cake with a skewer, pipe outlines with frosting, spread or pipe frosting into shapes.

Prancer

2 x 340g packets buttercake mix
2 quantities Vienna cream
brown colouring
2 licorice straps
assorted sweets

Make cakes according to directions on packets. Spread mixture into 2 greased 20cm x 30cm lamington pans. Bake in moderate oven for about 30 minutes or until firm; cool on wire racks.

STEP 1

Place cakes together, use paper pattern to cut out cake.

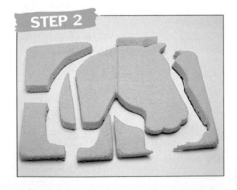

STEP 2

Assemble cake on prepared board, join with a little Vienna cream. Tint two-thirds of remaining cream brown, spread evenly over cake, except for mane. Use plain remaining cream for mane. Use licorice strips and pieces for eye, nostril and bridle; arrange on cake with sweets.

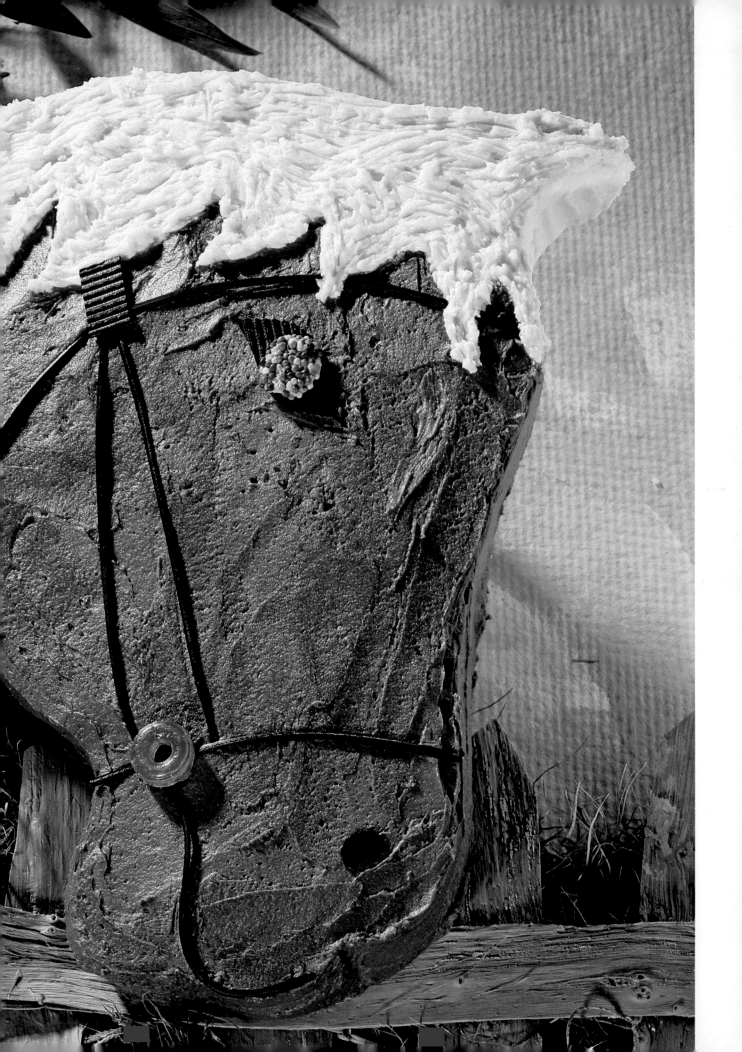

Red Alert Robot

2 x 340g packets buttercake mix
2 quantities Vienna cream
black and red colourings
assorted sweets
2 licorice straps

Make cakes according to directions on packets. Spread mixture into 2 greased 20cm x 30cm lamington pans. Bake in moderate oven for about 30 minutes or until firm; cool on wire racks.

STEP 2

Use cake scraps to make arms, secure to body with a little more cream. Tint half the remaining cream grey with black colouring, spread evenly over head, legs and hands. Tint remaining cream red; spread evenly over chest and arms. Use sweets and licorice to decorate cake.

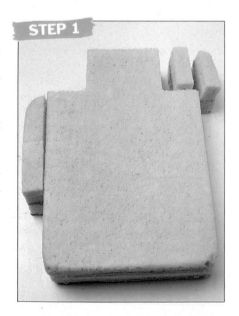

STEP 1

Sandwich cakes together on prepared board, using a little Vienna cream. Cut head shape from end of cake.

Roller-Skate

3 x 340g packets buttercake mix
1½ quantities fluffy frosting
4 plain doughnuts
rose pink and black colourings
2 licorice straps
1 pair long bootlaces
black jelly beans
musk sticks

Make cakes according to directions on packets. Spread mixture into 2 greased 20cm x 30cm lamington pans. Bake in moderate oven for about 40 minutes or until firm; cool on wire racks.

STEP 2

Place the larger pieces of cake and 1 triangle together.

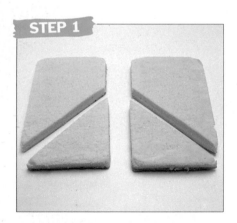

STEP 1

Cut a triangle from the corner of each cake, as shown.

STEP 3

Cut cakes to shape of roller-skate, join cake pieces together on prepared board with a little frosting. Cut 7cm circle from remaining triangle of cake for front stopper. Secure stopper and doughnuts to roller-skate with a little more frosting.

Tint one-third of remaining frosting pink, spread over top, side and wheels of skate. Tint ½ cup frosting black, use for front stopper. Spread remaining white frosting over cake. Decorate cake with licorice strips, cut out licorice letters and decorations. Use laces, pieces of jelly beans and musk sticks to finish cake.

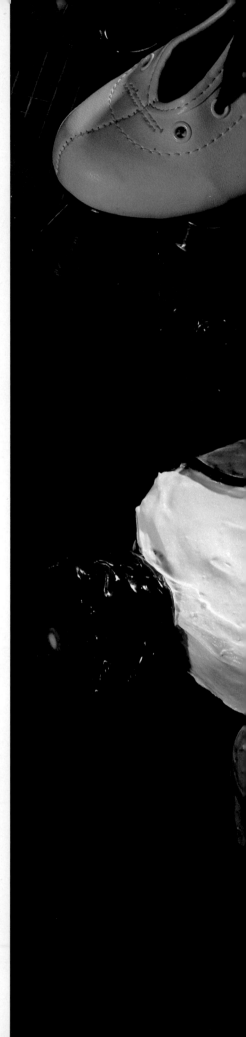

Sammy

We used quandong jellies for water (see Glossary).

3 x 340g packets buttercake mix
2 quantities Vienna cream
black, orange, blue, green and rose
pink colourings
25cm gathered cotton lace
4 licorice straps
1 white marshmallow

Make cakes according to directions on packets. Spread mixture into 3 greased 20cm x 30cm lamington pans. Bake in moderate oven for about 30 minutes or until firm; cool on wire racks.

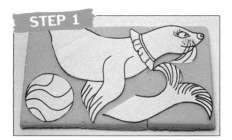

STEP 1

Place cakes side by side, use paper pattern to cut out seal and ball.

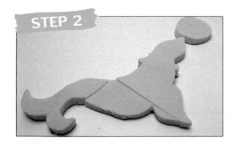

STEP 2

Assemble cake pieces on prepared board, join with a little Vienna cream.

Tint two-thirds of the remaining cream grey with black colouring, spread evenly over cake, roughen with a fork. Divide remaining cream into 4 portions, colour each portion with remaining colours, use to decorate ball.

Place lace around Sammy's neck. Use thin licorice strips to outline and decorate cake and ball. Use licorice and small pieces of marshmallow to make eye and tip of nose.

Silly Scarecrow

2 x 340g packets buttercake mix
2 quantities Vienna cream
black, brown, green and red
    colourings
1 licorice strap
assorted sweets
50g packet cheese-flavoured Twisties
1 wafer biscuit

Make cakes according to directions on packets. Spread 1½ cups of mixture into greased 8cm x 26cm bar pan, 2 cups into greased deep 17cm round cake pan, remainder into greased 23cm square slab pan. Bake cakes in moderate oven for about 25 minutes or until firm; cool cakes on wire racks.

STEP 2

Assemble cake pieces on prepared board, join with a little Vienna cream. Tint ⅔ cup of remaining cream grey with black colouring, spread over legs. Tint 1 cup cream pale brown, spread over face, neck, hands and feet. Tint ⅔ cup cream green; use for hat. Tint remaining cream red, use for coat. Decorate cake with remaining ingredients.

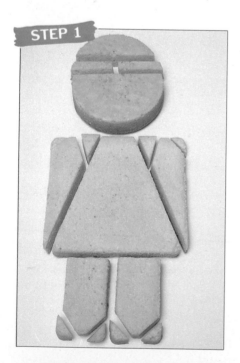

STEP 1

Level tops of cakes so they are all the same height. Position round cake above square cake, cut bar cake in half, place in position for legs. Cut cakes as shown.

Skull & Crossbones

3 x 340g packets buttercake mix
3 quantities fluffy frosting
2 egg shell halves
assorted sweets
1 licorice strap

Make cakes according to directions on packets. Spread mixture into 2 greased 20cm x 30cm lamington pans. Bake in moderate oven for about 40 minutes or until firm; cool on wire racks.

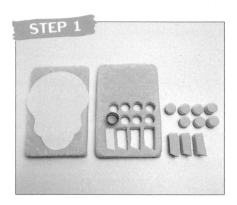

STEP 1

Use paper pattern to cut skull from 1 cake. Cut 8 x 2cm rounds from remaining cake for ends of bones. Cut 4 rectangles for bones from same cake.

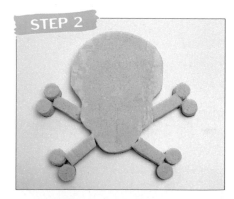

STEP 2

Assemble cake pieces on prepared board, join with a little frosting. Cover cake with remaining frosting. Decorate cake with remaining ingredients.

Background painting from Prop Art, Sydney

Snow Skis

5 x 340g packets buttercake mix
1½ quantities fluffy frosting
2 quantities Vienna cream
green, red, blue and yellow colourings
2 licorice straps

Make 3 cakes according to directions on packets. Divide the mixture between 3 greased 20cm x 30cm lamington pans. Bake in moderate oven for about 30 minutes or until firm; cool on wire racks.

Make remaining cakes according to directions on packets. Divide mixture between 4 greased 8cm x 26cm bar pans, bake in moderate oven for about 30 minutes or until firm; cool on wire racks.

STEP 1

Trim edges from lamington cakes, join cakes with a little fluffy frosting on prepared board. Spread cakes evenly with frosting.

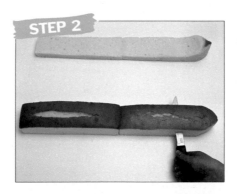

STEP 2

Trim edges from bar cakes; cut cakes to shape of skis, join cakes with a little Vienna cream. Tint half the remaining cream green. Divide remaining cream into 3 portions, tint each portion with remaining colours. Spread cream onto skis. Position skis on frosted cakes. Decorate with licorice strips.

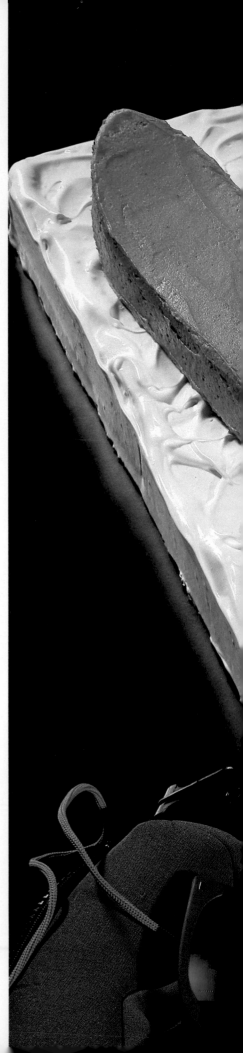

Snowy

2 x 340g packets buttercake mix
1½ quantities fluffy frosting
red and blue colourings
1 small carrot, peeled
black sweets
1 licorice strap
ribbon

Make cakes according to directions on packets. Bake cakes in 2 greased 20cm x 30cm lamington pans. Bake in moderate oven for about 30 minutes or until firm; cool on wire racks.

Cut cakes as shown.

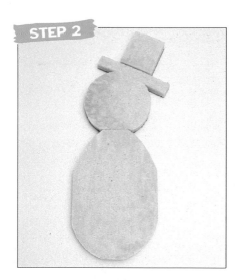

Assemble pieces of cake on prepared board, join with a little fluffy frosting. Tint 1 cup of remaining frosting pink, tint another ½ cup frosting blue. Spread frostings over cake. Decorate cake with carrot, sweets, licorice and ribbon.

Space Ship

2 x 340g packets buttercake mix
1½ quantities fluffy frosting
pink and white marshmallows
2 long thin licorice tubes
assorted sweets
silver cachous
1 sheet gelatine

Make cakes according to directions on packets. Spread mixture into 2 greased 20cm x 30cm lamington pans. Bake in moderate oven for about 30 minutes or until firm; cool on wire racks.

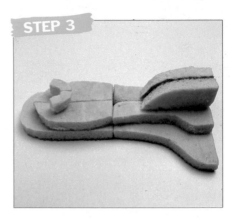

STEP 3

Position large centre pieces of cakes on prepared board, join with a little fluffy frosting. Use remaining pieces of trimmed cake for tail of space ship and cockpit, secure with a little more frosting. Spread remaining frosting over cake. Position marshmallows on back of cake. Decorate cake with licorice, sweets and cachous.

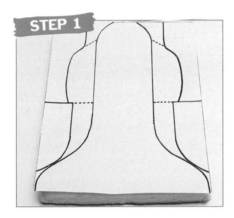

STEP 1

Place cakes together; use paper pattern to cut out cake.

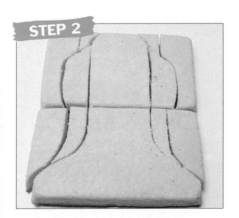

STEP 2

Picture shows cut out cakes.

STEP 4

Cut out sheet gelatine to make cockpit for space ship.

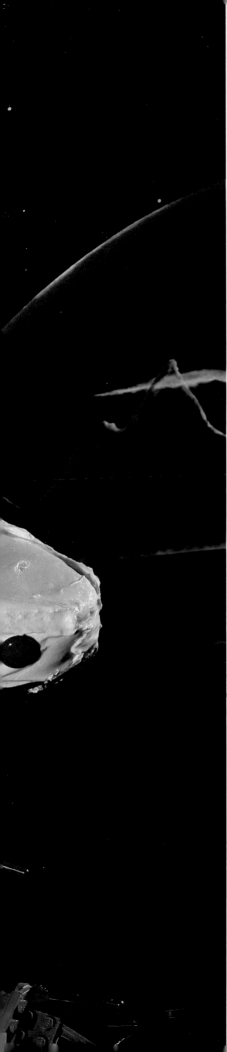

Space Station

2 x 340g packets buttercake mix
2 sponge rolls
2 quantities Vienna cream
green colouring
assorted sweets
1 licorice strap
3 snowballs

Make cakes according to directions on packets. Spread mixture into greased deep 28cm round cake pan. Bake in moderate oven for about 45 minutes or until firm; cool on wire rack.

STEP 2

Cut sponge rolls in half, cut 2cm slice from 1 half; discard slice.

Cut small ring of cake into 3 pieces. Position large ring of cake and pieces of roll on prepared board.

STEP 1

Cut 12cm round from centre of cake. Cut 6cm round from centre of the large round, discard small round of cake.

STEP 3

Secure the 3 remaining pieces of cake on large ring of cake, using a little Vienna cream. Tint cream green, spread over cake. Decorate cake with sweets, strips of licorice and snowballs.

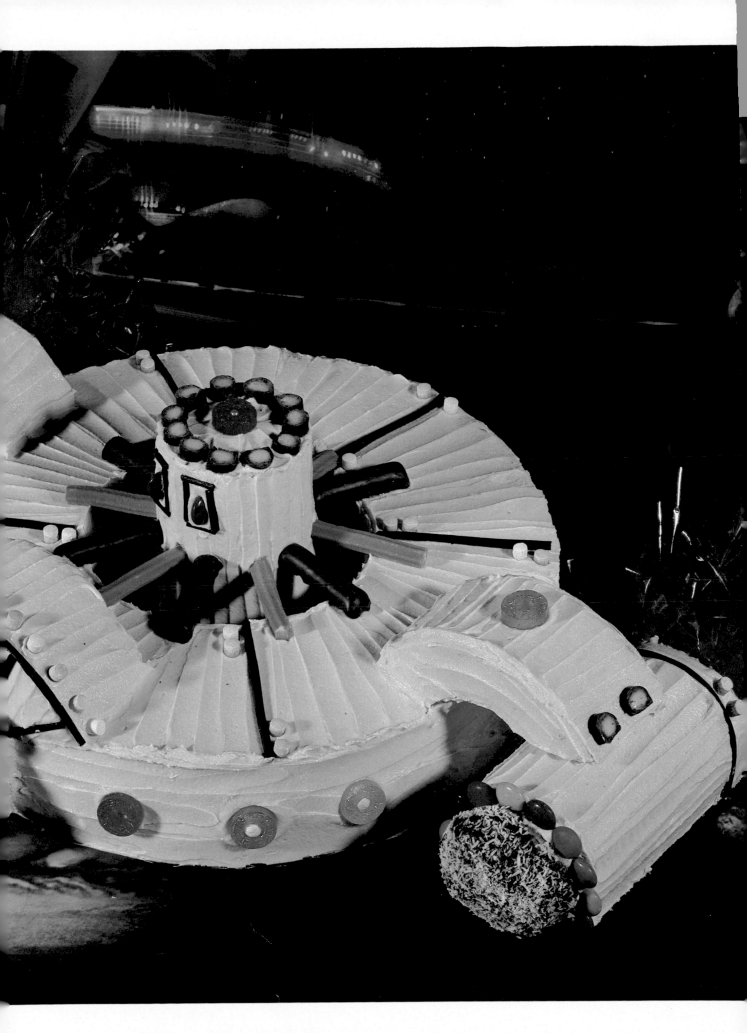

the AMAZING SPIDER-MAN

2 x 340g packets buttercake mix
1 quantity fluffy frosting
black and red colourings

Make cakes according to directions on packets. Spread mixture into greased 32cm long oval cake pan. Bake in moderate oven for about 40 minutes or until firm; cool on wire rack.

Trim sides from cake, position on prepared board. Reserve ⅓ cup fluffy frosting for eyes. Tint 1½ cups of frosting black. Tint remaining frosting red. Spread red frosting over cake except for eyes. Spread half the black frosting and reserved white frosting over eyes. Pipe remaining black frosting over cake.

Spiky Echidna

340g packet buttercake mix
1 Bounty Bar
1 quantity chocolate Vienna cream
2 x 125g packets chocolate mint sticks
4 black jelly beans
1 licorice strap

Make cake according to directions on packet. Spread mixture into greased and floured aluminium steamer (8 cup capacity, or with 18cm diameter top and 9½cm depth). Bake cake in moderate oven for about 50 minutes or until firm; cool on wire rack.

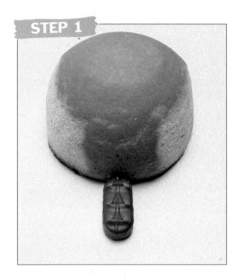

STEP 1

Level top of cake, position cake on prepared board. Trim sides of cake, trim cake to a slight point at 1 end. Place Bounty Bar in position for nose, secure with a little Vienna cream. Spread cake and bar evenly with remaining cream.

STEP 2

Cut chocolate mint sticks in half, trim ends to points. Decorate cake with sticks and jelly beans. Use licorice for tongue.

Sporty Shoe

4 x 340g packets buttercake mix
2 quantities Vienna cream
purple and green colourings
3 licorice straps
1 long thin licorice tube

Make cakes according to directions on packets. Divide mixture between 4 greased 23cm square slab pans. Bake cakes in moderate oven for about 35 minutes or until firm; cool on wire racks.

STEP 2

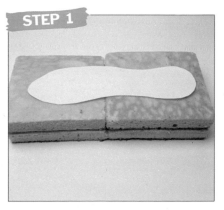

STEP 1

Place cakes together, use paper pattern to cut shoe shape.

Cut front of shoe to shape; use scraps of cake to build up front of shoe. Hollow out cake for inside of shoe. Use more scraps of cake to build up side of shoe.

Join pieces of cake together on prepared board with a little Vienna cream. Spread two-thirds of cream over cake, except inside of shoe.

Tint 2 tablespoons of the remaining cream purple, tint remaining cream green; reserve 2 tablespoons. Spread green cream over inside of shoe. Use reserved green and purple cream for piping. Decorate cake with licorice pieces and licorice tube for lace.

Shoe box from Prop Art, Sydney

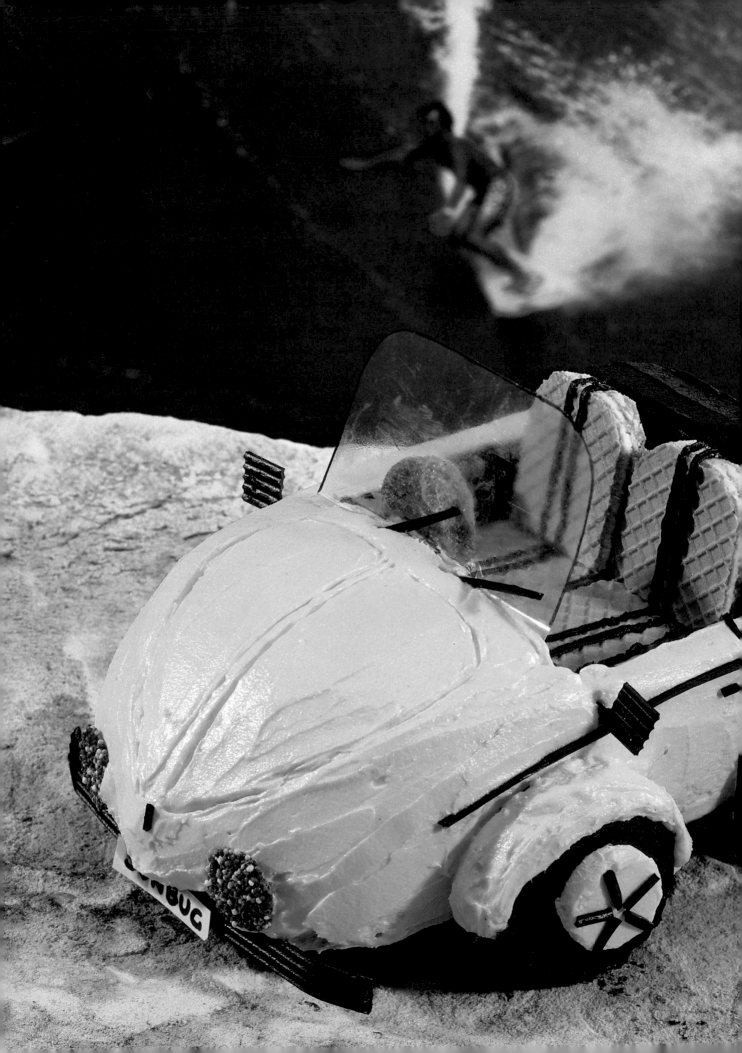

Sun Bug

2 x 340g packets buttercake mix
2 quantities Vienna cream
black and yellow colourings
8 round chocolate-coated biscuits
2 yellow marshmallows, halved
2 licorice straps
4 wafer biscuits
4 freckles
1 black jelly ring
clear thick plastic

Make cakes according to directions on packets. Spread 1½ cups of mixture into greased 8cm x 26cm bar pan. Spread remaining mixture into greased 15cm x 25cm loaf pan. Bake cakes in moderate oven for about 25 minutes, remove bar cake. Bake loaf cake further 25 minutes or until firm; cool on wire racks.

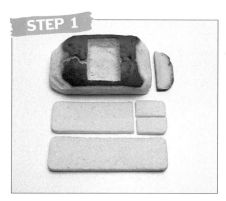

STEP 1

Level bar cake, split in half lengthways, cut 2 pieces from end of 1 half. Cut loaf cake into shape, as shown.

STEP 2

Secure spoiler to back of car with toothpicks. Position 2 small pieces of bar cake at back of seat, secure with a little Vienna cream. Position large piece of remaining bar cake on prepared board, use a little more cream to position body of car on top of bar cake. Remaining piece of bar cake is not used for this cake.

Tint ⅔ cup of the remaining cream black, reserve ¼ cup. Tint remaining cream yellow; reserve ⅓ cup. Spread black cream evenly over inside of bug and bonnet, spread yellow cream evenly over outside of bug.

Sandwich 2 chocolate-coated biscuits together for wheels, cover 1 side of each wheel with half the reserved black cream; position on cake.

Spread marshmallows with a little of the reserved yellow cream, place on wheels, decorate with licorice pieces. Spread remaining yellow cream over tops of wheels for mudguards.

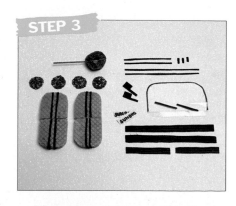

STEP 3

Trim wafer biscuits to shape of seats, pipe with remaining black cream, position in car. Decorate car with licorice pieces, sweets and plastic for windscreen.

Tales of Mopsy & Topsy

3 x 340g packets buttercake mix
2 quantities Vienna cream
rose pink colouring
2 tablespoons cocoa
1 metre ribbon
13cm x 22cm greeting card

Make cakes according to directions on packets. Spread mixture into 2 greased 20cm x 30cm lamington pans. Bake in moderate oven for about 40 minutes or until firm; cool on wire racks.

STEP 2

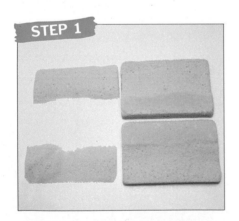

STEP 1

Place cakes side by side, cut a slice at an angle from each cake as shown.

Position cake on prepared board. Use cake scraps to make centre of book, secure in position with Vienna cream.

Reserve ½ cup of the remaining cream. Tint remaining cream pink, spread evenly over cake. Using a fork, mark pages of book. Stir sifted cocoa into reserved cream, use for piping border and writing. Position ribbon and card just before serving, as cream will stain both.

Chapter 7

Mopsy, Topsy
and all their
brother and
sister kittens.
~ page 38 ~

37~

Tangles

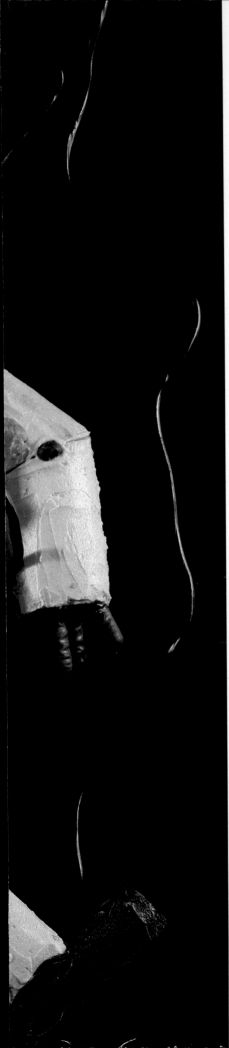

340g packet buttercake mix
1 sponge roll, halved
8 sponge rollettes
2 quantities Vienna cream
brown, green, yellow and black
    colourings
6 long thin licorice tubes
chocolate sticks
1 licorice strap
2 pink marshmallows
pink cake sprinkles
assorted sweets
blue feathers

Make cake according to directions on packet. Spread mixture into greased 15cm x 25cm loaf pan. Bake in moderate oven for about 40 minutes or until firm; cool on wire rack.

STEP 2

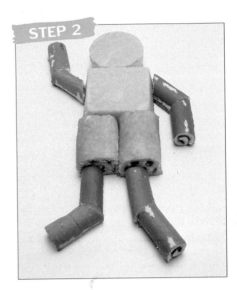

STEP 1

Level cake, cut a circle the width of the cake from the cake. Cut a square from the remaining piece of cake.

Position cake pieces, sponge roll halves and rollettes on prepared board, secure with a little Vienna cream.

Tint half the remaining cream pale brown for body. Tint ½ cup cream green for trousers, and another ½ cup cream yellow for shirt. Tint remaining cream black for feet. Spread creams evenly over cake, use licorice tubes for puppet's string. Decorate the cake with the remaining ingredients.

Puppet from Fantastic Toys & Models

Teddy Bear

3 x 340g packets buttercake mix
1 quantity Vienna cream
1 tablespoon cocoa
brown colouring
assorted sweets
1 licorice strap

Make cakes according to directions on packets. Spread mixture into 2 greased 20cm x 30cm lamington pans. Bake in moderate oven for about 40 minutes or until firm; cool on wire racks.

STEP 2

STEP 1

Place cakes side by side, use paper pattern to cut out bear.

Position pieces of cake on prepared board, secure with a little Vienna cream. Use quarter of remaining cream for paws, mouth and tummy. Stir sifted cocoa into remaining cream, add colouring to make brown. Spread brown cream over cake; roughen with fork. Decorate cake with sweets and licorice strips.

Treasure Chart

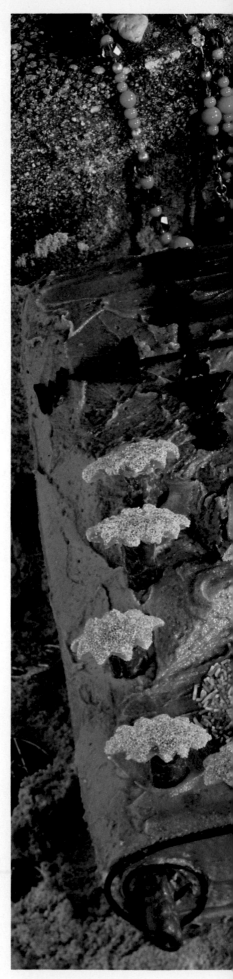

85g packet quandong jelly crystals
1 cup boiling water
3 x 340g packets buttercake mix
2 quantities Vienna cream
1 tablespoon cocoa
2 licorice straps
100g dark Toblerone
100g milk Toblerone
100g white Toblerone
250g packet chocolate-coated
    honeycomb pieces
assorted sweets
yellow and orange cake sprinkles

Make jelly as directed on packet using the
1 cup of boiling water, pour into lamington
pan; cool, refrigerate until set. Make cakes
according to directions on packets.
Spread mixture into 2 greased 20cm x
30cm lamington pans. Bake in moderate
oven for about 40 minutes or until firm;
cool on wire racks.

STEP 1

Trim cakes; shape opposite long sides
as shown.

STEP 2

Join cakes with a little Vienna cream on
prepared board. Stir sifted cocoa into
remaining cream, spread evenly over
cakes. Use licorice, chopped jelly and
remaining ingredients to decorate cake.

*Treasure chest from Gallery Nomad; jewellery from
Rose Stokes Antiques*

114

Villainous Vampire

**2 x 340g packets buttercake mix
2 quantities Vienna cream
black, red and brown colourings
assorted sweets
1 licorice strap
small round black sweets
1 metre ribbon**

Make cakes according to directions on packets. Spread mixture into greased 32cm long oval cake pan. Bake in moderate oven for about 40 minutes or until firm; cool on wire rack.

STEP 2

Use sweets to make teeth for vampire. Decorate cake with remaining ingredients.

STEP 1

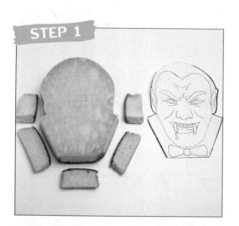

Use paper pattern to cut out cake; position cake on prepared board. Spread 1 cup of Vienna cream evenly over face and ears. Tint 1½ cups of remaining cream black, reserve 2 tablespoons; spread black cream over hair and collar.

Tint ½ cup of remaining cream red, use for lips, blood droplets and for piping in lines for bloodshot eyes. Tint remaining cream pale brown, use to pipe facial lines. Pipe reserved black cream around eyes; fill in nostrils and mouth.

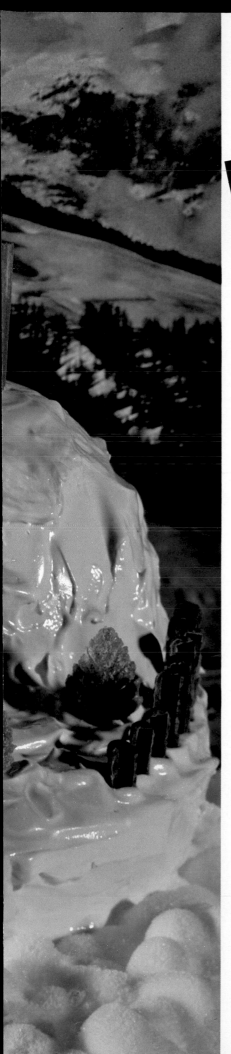

Winter Wonderland

We used dariole and timbale moulds to create different heights and shapes for the ski slope. Several patty cakes stacked together will also give good results.

2 x 340g packets buttercake mix
1½ quantities fluffy frosting
1 licorice strap
2 wafer biscuits
assorted sweets

Make cakes according to directions on packets. Spread half the mixture into greased deep 28cm round cake pan. Bake in moderate oven for about 20 minutes or until firm; cool on wire rack.

Half fill 2 greased moulds (½ cup and 1 cup capacity) with some of the remaining cake mixture. Spread remaining mixture into greased and floured aluminium pudding steamer (6 cup capacity, or with 15cm diameter top and 9½cm depth).

Bake cakes in moderate oven for about 15 minutes for the smallest cake, about 25 minutes for the medium cake and about 35 minutes for the largest cake, or until firm; cool on wire racks.

Level cakes, assemble on prepared board with a little frosting. Cut out small piece of cake for ski-slope.

Secure ski-slope with a little more frosting. Reserve 2 tablespoons frosting, spread remaining frosting over cake. Decorate cake with remaining ingredients. Use reserved frosting for signs.

119

Wobbly Wombat

3 x 340g packets buttercake mix
2 quantities chocolate Vienna cream
1 oval chocolate-coated biscuit
2 black jelly beans
2 small chocolate discs
1 square chocolate after-dinner mint
1 licorice strap

Make cakes according to directions on packets. Two-thirds fill 2 greased muffin pans (⅓ cup capacity) with mixture; two-thirds fill greased deep 17cm round cake pan with mixture. Bake these cakes in moderate oven for about 20 minutes, remove small cakes. Bake larger cake for about further 25 minutes or until firm; cool cakes on wire racks.

Two-thirds fill greased and floured aluminium pudding steamer (6 cup capacity, or with 15cm diameter top and 9½cm depth) with mixture. Spread remaining mixture into greased and floured Dolly Varden cake pan (10 cup capacity, or with 18cm diameter top and 15cm depth). Bake these cakes in moderate oven for about 35 minutes, remove pudding steamer. Bake remaining cake for about further 10 minutes or until firm; cool cakes on wire racks.

STEP 1

Level the 3 large cakes, join together with a little Vienna cream on prepared board. Cut small cakes in half, secure in position with a little cream for legs.

STEP 2

Spread cake evenly with remaining cream, roughen cream with a fork to represent wombat's coat. Decorate with remaining ingredients.

121

Wrist Watch

3 x 340g packets buttercake mix
2 quantities Vienna cream
red, brown and black colourings
1 licorice strap

Make cakes according to directions on packets. Spread one-third of the mixture into greased deep 20cm round cake pan. Spread remaining mixture into greased and floured aluminium pudding steamer (16 cup capacity, or with 24cm diameter top and 11½cm depth). Bake cakes in moderate oven for about 40 minutes, remove round cake. Bake remaining cake about further 25 minutes or until firm; cool on wire rack.

STEP 2

Cut 15cm circle from round cake, discard trimmings.

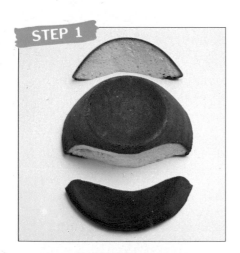

STEP 1

Level cakes, cut sides from pudding-shaped cake, cut small circle from cake trimmings for watch winder.

STEP 3

Secure round piece of cake on large cake with a little Vienna cream. Position cake on prepared board. Spread quarter of remaining cream evenly over watch face; reserve ¼ cup cream. Tint half the remaining cream red, tint remaining cream pale brown. Secure winder to watch face with a little cream.

Spread creams evenly over remaining cake, including winder. Decorate watch face with strips of licorice. Tint reserved cream black, use for piping numerals onto watch face.

Hints for success

Follow our guidelines for terrific results whether you copy our cakes or create your own designs.

• We used White Wings Golden Buttercake Cake Mix throughout this book for consistency; use any flavour of your choice. It is important that the packet be fresh; check the "use by" date.
• We used an electric mixer to beat the mixture until it was thick and creamy; follow directions on packets.
• A large mixing bowl will hold up to 4 packet mixes. It is best to mix single packets in a small bowl, 2 or more packets in medium to large bowls.
NOTE: If you prefer to make your own cakes, see recipes later in this section; we include a Cornflour Sponge for people allergic to gluten in regular flour.

GREASING CAKE PANS

We used a pastry brush to grease cake pans lightly but evenly with a little melted butter. Some people prefer to line the base of cake pans with greaseproof or baking paper; it's a matter of choice. We dusted greased aluminium pudding steamers and Dolly Varden pans with flour, then shook out the excess.

BAKING CAKES TOGETHER

It is easy to bake cakes together on the same shelf or on different shelves. The important thing is that the cake pans do not touch each other, or the sides of the oven, or the door when it is closed. If baking cakes on the same shelf, change the positions of the pans about halfway through baking time.

If baking cakes on different shelves, be sure there will be enough room for the lower cakes to rise without touching the bottom of the upper shelves. Change the cakes from the lower to upper shelf positions halfway through baking time for even browning.

When small cakes are being baked with larger cakes which take longer to bake, position the small ones in the best baking position towards the front of the oven, then move the large cakes into that position to complete their baking time.

When 2 or more cakes are being baked in the oven at the same time, the baking times may be slightly longer than specified in recipes. When properly cooked, packet mixes and sponges feel firm to touch and are slightly shrunken from the sides of the pan. There should not be any need to test with a skewer. Home-made butter cakes feel firm, too.

However, if in doubt, test by inserting a metal skewer into the cake; if any mixture clings to the skewer the cake needs a little more baking time.

LEVELLING CAKES

Most cake mixtures rise unevenly or to a peak, particularly those cooked in loaf, bar and round pans. In most cases, the top needs to be cut off so the cake will sit flat or join smoothly to other cakes.

AVOIDING CRUMBS

Our cakes are simple to decorate but crumbs can be troublesome when they get into the Vienna cream or fluffy frosting and make it bumpy.

To keep the cake as neat as possible, bake the cake a day before you decorate it. After cooling, keep it in an airtight container in the refrigerator overnight.

Decorate the cake while it is cold or, if you think you are going to take more than about 30 minutes, freeze the cake, uncovered, for 30 minutes, then decorate. This will not eliminate the crumb problem but will certainly help.

VIENNA CREAM

This is a basic Vienna cream recipe; the flavour can be varied by adding finely grated rind of orange, lemon, lime, mandarin, etc, or any essence added to your taste. A coffee flavour is pleasant, too. Warm the milk and add 2 teaspoons instant coffee powder, stir to dissolve, cool to room temperature before using.

If a lot of liquid colouring has been added to this cream, it may look a little curdly. Simply beat in a tablespoon or 2 more of sifted icing sugar.

125g butter
1½ cups icing sugar
2 tablespoons milk

Have butter at room temperature, cream butter in small bowl with electric mixer until as white as possible, gradually beat in half the sifted icing sugar, all the milk, then the remaining icing sugar. Flavour and colour as required.
CHOCOLATE VARIATION: Sift in ⅓ cup cocoa with the icing sugar.

FLUFFY FROSTING

1 cup sugar
⅓ cup water
2 egg whites

Combine sugar and water in small saucepan, stir constantly with a wooden spoon over heat, without boiling, until sugar is dissolved. Boil, uncovered, without stirring, for 3 to 5 minutes or until slightly thick but not coloured.

If a candy thermometer is available, the syrup should reach 114°C (240°F) when it is ready to use.

Otherwise, test the syrup by dropping 1 teaspoon into a cup of cold water. The syrup should form a ball of soft sticky toffee when rolled gently between your fingertips.

If testing syrup in water, remove pan from heat when syrup falls from spoon in a heavy drop; allow bubbles to subside, then test in cold water. The syrup should not change colour; if it does, it has been cooked for too long and you will have to throw out that batch and start again.

While syrup is boiling, beat egg whites in small bowl with electric mixer until stiff, keep beating (or whites will deflate) while syrup is reaching the correct temperature.

When syrup is ready, allow bubbles to subside, pour a very thin stream onto the egg whites while mixer is operating on medium speed.

If syrup is added too quickly to the egg whites, frosting will not thicken. Continue beating and adding syrup until all syrup is used. Continue to beat until frosting stands in stiff peaks (frosting should be only warm at this stage).

Tint, if desired, by beating food colouring through while mixing or by stirring through with spatula at the end.

Frosting can also be flavoured with a little of any essence of your choice.

For best results, frosting should be applied to a cake on the day it is to be served, while frosting is beautifully soft with a marshmallow consistency. The cake can be frosted the day before; however, frosting will become crisp because it has dried out a little and will lose its glossy appearance, much like a meringue.

Make sure to frost cake around the base near the board; this will form a seal and help keep the cake fresh.

CHOOSING VIENNA CREAM OR FLUFFY FROSTING

We used either Vienna cream or fluffy frosting, depending on the effect we fancied. Vienna cream is a little harder to spread than fluffy frosting but you can work with Vienna cream longer than with frosting, which tends to set. Fluffy frosting is good for fluffy or snowy effects but it is fairly difficult to make smooth.

The choice of cream or frosting really depends on your taste. However, because Vienna cream is based on butter, the yellow colour of the butter will alter the colouring you add. For example, if you

add rose pink, the cream tends to become salmon pink; if you add red it becomes apricot and so on. If you make fluffy frosting, you have a white base to colour from.

We used a small spatula for best results, and added an extra swirl of Vienna cream or fluffy frosting to cover any imperfections.

HOW TO MAKE AND USE A PAPER PIPING BAG

Some cakes need a little piping to complete them, and it's simple to make a piping bag from greaseproof or baking paper. You don't need tubes, simply cut a tiny hole at the piping end.

Cut triangle from paper and twist into cone shape, as shown.

Fill cone with Vienna cream or frosting; here we use Vienna cream.

Fold end of cone over to keep cream contained inside paper bag.

Hold bag for piping as shown; squeeze gently but firmly.

PREPARING CAKE BOARDS

We have indicated in recipes when to position cakes on boards as most people will want to present the cakes on a board, platter or plate, etc. Our cakes have been put into an appropriate setting to indicate to you how to "set the scene" for a particular theme or party.

Use Masonite or similar board; check the cake pans or cut a paper pattern to help you get the right size. Allow extra space for frostings and decorations.

The board needs to be covered with some sort of greaseproof paper. Special paper is available from cake decorators suppliers (see Bakeware later in this section), or you can use certain gift paper such as a thin patterned aluminium foil. Kitchen-type aluminium foil is also ideal.

To cover round board, snip paper shape at intervals, as shown. Fold over and tape securely to board.

Neaten back with paper circle glued in position, as shown.

To cover square board, cut paper to size, neaten corners and tape securely to board, as shown.

Neaten back with paper square glued into position, as shown.

SWEETS AND DECORATIONS

We used a large variety of readily available sweets and other edible goodies on our cakes. Use finished cake photographs as a guide to what to buy. Most commercial sweets and biscuits, etc, recommended in this book have been described in the Glossary.

If placing trimmings, such as lace, braid and ribbon, etc, on a cake with Vienna cream, position them at the last minute as the butter from the cream will discolour any fabric. If using these trimmings on a cake with fluffy frosting, it is best to position them before the frosting is set.

COLOURINGS

We used good-quality liquid and powdered vegetable food colourings made by Gold Badge and Corella. These are available from cake decorators suppliers (see Bakeware later in this section) and some health food stores.

For bold strong colours such as reds and blacks, powdered colourings give best results, as they do not add extra liquid to the Vienna cream or fluffy frosting.

HOW TO TOAST SESAME SEEDS AND DESICCATED COCONUT

Place coconut or sesame seeds in heavy-based frying pan, stir over moderately high heat until golden brown. Immediately remove from pan, cool to room temperature before using. Keep any leftovers in airtight container in refrigerator.

HOW TO TOAST SHREDDED OR FLAKED COCONUT

Spread coconut on flat oven tray (we used a shallow Swiss roll pan); toast in moderate oven for about 5 minutes or until golden brown. Cool to room temperature before using. Keep any leftover coconut in airtight container in refrigerator.

HOW TO COLOUR COCONUT

Place coconut in plastic bag, add a drop or two of liquid colouring, knead colouring through coconut by pressing and pushing the bag. Keep leftover coconut in airtight container in refrigerator.

3 BASIC CAKE RECIPES

Although we used packet mixes for consistency of size and texture, you can make any cake of your choice, or follow 1 of the following recipes.

The Basic Butter Cake, Best Ever Sponge and the Cornflour Sponge are given in quantities equivalent, in volume, to 1 packet White Wings Golden Buttercake Cake Mix. So, if 1 of our decorated cake recipes requires 2 packets buttercake mix, double whichever recipe you choose. The baking times for the packet mix and the recipes given below are very similar; the sponges usually take a little less baking time.

BASIC BUTTER CAKE

125g butter
1 teaspoon vanilla essence
¾ cup castor sugar
2 eggs
1½ cups self-raising flour
½ cup milk

Cream butter, essence and sugar in small bowl with electric mixer until light and fluffy; beat in 1 egg at a time, until combined. Stir in sifted flour and milk in 2 batches. Spread mixture into prepared pan. Bake in moderate oven for specified cooking time (see note above) or until cake is firm; cool on wire rack.

BEST EVER SPONGE

This recipe does not contain any liquid.

3 eggs
½ cup castor sugar
¼ cup cornflour
¼ cup plain flour
¼ cup self-raising flour

Eggs should be at room temperature. Beat whole eggs in small bowl with electric mixer on moderately high speed until thick and creamy; about 7 minutes. Add sugar 1 tablespoon at a time, beating after each addition until sugar is dissolved. Sift dry ingredients together 3 times. When sugar is dissolved transfer mixture to larger bowl. Sift flours over egg mixture, fold in lightly. Spread mixture into prepared pan. Bake in moderate oven for specified cooking time (see note above) or until firm; cool on wire rack.

GLUTEN-FREE CORNFLOUR SPONGE

This recipe does not contain any liquid. We used Fielders wheaten cornflour in this recipe; it is ideal for gluten-free diets.

4 eggs
½ cup castor sugar
1 cup cornflour

Beat eggs in medium bowl with electric mixer for about 7 minutes, or until thick and creamy. Gradually add sugar, beating well after each addition. Beat until sugar is dissolved. Sift cornflour 3 times, then sift over egg mixture. Gently fold flour into egg mixture. Spread mixture evenly into prepared pan. Bake in moderate oven for specified cooking time (see note left), or until firm; cool on wire rack.

BAKEWARE

Most of the cake pans used in this book are made by Namco and are available from most department stores.

Any special-shaped pans, such as the oval or Dolly Varden, are available from cake decorators suppliers. For more information, write (with stamped, self-addressed envelope) to:

Cake Decorators Supplies, 770 George Street, Sydney, 2000; or telephone (02) 212 4050.

Oval shapes can also be cut from either square or round cakes, or a combination of both. For example, to make a 32cm long oval cake, bake a 23cm round and a 23cm square cake, cut the round cake in half and position the square cake between the 2 halves; trim to shape.

A Dolly Varden shape can be made by baking the cake in an aluminium pudding steamer then trimming the cake to the shape required.

Some cakes require deep round shapes, for which we've used aluminium pudding steamers. To help you choose the right shape, size is indicated in recipes by fluid capacity in metric cups as well as diameter and depth. To measure the fluid capacity, fill the steamer to the brim with metric cups of water.

THE BAKEWARE WE USED

1: deep 15cm square cake pan

2: 23cm square slab pan

3: 20cm x 30cm lamington pan

4: 14cm x 21cm loaf pan

5: 15cm x 25cm loaf pan

6: deep 17cm round cake pan

7: deep 20cm round cake pan

8: deep 23cm round cake pan

9: deep 28cm round cake pan

10: muffin pan (1/3 cup capacity)

11: timbale mould (1/2 cup capacity)

12: dariole mould (1 cup capacity)

13: 8cm x 26cm bar pan

14: 25cm long oval cake pan

15: 32cm long oval cake pan

16: Dolly Varden cake pan (10 cup capacity)

17: aluminium pudding steamer (6 cup capacity)

18: aluminium pudding steamer (8 cup capacity)

19: aluminium pudding steamer (9 cup capacity)

20: aluminium pudding steamer (11 cup capacity)

21: aluminium pudding steamer (16 cup capacity)

Note: all measurements are taken from the top of the pans.

Glossary

Some terms, names, and alternatives are included here to help everyone understand and use our recipes perfectly.

BISCUITS: cookies.
BOUNTY BAR: chocolate-coated coconut-flavoured fondant bar.
BUTTER: use salted or unsalted (sweet) butter; 125g is equal to 1 stick butter.
CACHOUS: small round cake-decorating sweets , available in silver, gold or colours.
CHOCOLATE:
COIN: gold, paper-wrapped, coin-shaped chocolate confection.
DARK: we used good cooking chocolate.
MINT BATONS: chocolate-coated thin sticks of peppermint-flavoured fondant. Chocolate sticks can be substituted.
STICKS: chocolate-coated biscuits about 4½cm long and 1cm wide.
TOP DECK: block of chocolate with milk chocolate base and white chocolate tops.
WHITE: we used Milky Bar, which is available in 50g, 200g and 250g blocks.
WHITE MELTS: compounded white chocolate discs 2½cm in diameter.
COCOA: cocoa powder.
COCONUT: use desiccated coconut unless otherwise stated.
FLAKED: coconut flesh that has been flaked and dried.
SHREDDED: thin strips of coconut.
COLOURINGS: we used concentrated liquid vegetable food colourings and edible powder colourings.
CORNFLOUR: cornstarch. Fielders make a pure wheaten cornflour; it is ideal for gluten-free diets.
ESSENCE: extract.
FLAKE: light flaky 30g milk chocolate bar.
FLOUR:
PLAIN: also known as all-purpose flour.
SELF-RAISING: substitute plain flour and baking powder in the proportion of ¾ metric cup plain flour to 2 level metric teaspoons baking powder. Sift together several times before using. If using an 8oz measuring cup, use 1 cup plain flour to 2 level teaspoons baking powder.
FRECKLES: chocolate discs covered with hundreds and thousands.
GLUTEN: is the protein in flour that provides the elasticity and structure in ordinary bread; some people are allergic to gluten. See our Cornflour Sponge in Hints for Success section.
GOLDEN ROUGH: 20g chocolate and coconut disc, 7cm in diameter.

HUNDREDS AND THOUSANDS: nonpareils
ICE MAGIC: a liquid compounded chocolate which sets at a cold temperature.
JELLY CRYSTALS: fruit-flavoured gelatine crystals available from supermarkets.
JELLY RINGS: soft sugar-coated jubes in ring shapes.
LICORICE: an aniseed confection which comes in straps, tubes and twisted ropes.
ALLSORTS: layered sweets consisting of licorice and fondant.
BULLETS: small lengths of licorice coated in chocolate candy.
LONG THIN TUBES: about 40cm lengths.
STRAPS: about 40cm flat lengths.
MARSHMALLOWS: we used packaged round marshmallows coloured pink, white or yellow.
MILK: use full-cream homogenised milk.
MUSK STICK: musk-flavoured fondant.
QUANDONG JELLY CRYSTALS: blue jelly crystals flavoured with quandong fruit. If using this jelly to represent water, use only half the water recommended on the packet, refrigerate in a lamington pan, chop roughly when set. If quandong jelly is unavailable, lime jelly is a good substitute. If blue water is necessary, dissolve 1 tablespoon gelatine in ¼ cup water. Add 1 more cup water, then colour with blue colouring. Refrigerate until set, chop roughly.
SHEET GELATINE: available from some health food stores, delicatessens and gourmet food stores. It is an imported product.
SKEWERS, THIN WOODEN: we used bamboo satay skewers; these are available in several lengths.
SNOWBALL: marshmallow coated in chocolate and dipped in coconut.
SOFT ICING: ready-to-use cake fondant available in 500g packets and 375g tubs; the tubs are labelled "prepared icing".
SPEARMINT LEAVES: soft sugar-coated, leaf-shaped sweets.
SPONGE ROLL: we used a 250g Swiss roll filled with jam, or a 225g French roll filled with jam and cream.
SPONGE ROLLETTES: we used small sponge rolls about 9cm long filled with jam or jam and cream; these are generally purchased in 250g packets of 6.
SPRINKLES: different coloured cake sprinkles (nonpareils).
SUGAR:
CASTOR: fine granulated table sugar.
ICING: also known as confectioners' sugar or powdered sugar. We used icing sugar mixture, not pure icing sugar, unless otherwise specified.
PURE ICING: icing sugar which does not have cornflour added. Mostly used for royal icing and when handling fondant.
TWISTIES: cheese-flavoured snacks.
WAFER: thin crisp biscuit generally served with ice-cream and creamy desserts; can also be layered with sweet cream filling.
WAGON WHEEL: chocolate-coated cookie sandwich filled with jam and marshmallow; 9cm in diameter.